George B. Chase

**Lowndes of South Carolina**

An historical and genealogical Memoir

George B. Chase

**Lowndes of South Carolina**
*An historical and genealogical Memoir*

ISBN/EAN: 9783337063221

Printed in Europe, USA, Canada, Australia, Japan

Cover: Foto ©ninafisch / pixelio.de

More available books at **www.hansebooks.com**

# LOWNDES OF SOUTH CAROLINA

## An Historical and Genealogical Memoir

BY

GEORGE B. CHASE

A. M. HARV.

*"Nothing can we call our own — except our Dead"*

BOSTON
A. WILLIAMS AND COMPANY
1876

TO

MAJOR RAWLINS LOWNDES,

FORMERLY OF THE ARMY,

NOW OF HOPELAND, STAATSBURGH-ON-HUDSON,

THIS BRIEF MEMOIR OF HIS FAMILY

Is affectionately dedicated.

# INTRODUCTION.

The name of Lowndes, an uncommon one in the northern states of the Union, has been from an early period socially conspicuous throughout the southern country. The several families of Maryland, Virginia, and South Carolina cherished till recently the belief that they were all descendants in common of but one and the same branch of an ancient county family of England. This belief had in it much to appeal to the generous traits and hospitable character of the southern planters, who for a large part of each year lived in comparative retirement. They were always ready to assume, in the absence of anything to the contrary, that others of their name and class were of their kith and their kin, since they could thus claim the right to make them more welcome to their homes. While, too, such a belief gratified their love of hospitality, it enlarged their acquaintance, widened and deepened the current of their friendships, and increased the consideration and influence of their name.

Like others among the older English families of the South they accepted their family traditions, and believed them without question as they increased by repetition and friendly intercourse. Nor did they find their conviction of a wide-scattered kindred in the colonies shaken, even when the old family seals from different parts of the country indicated a separation of their ancestors in England, relatively as wide as their own settlements in the original colonies. Attaching its proper significance to heraldic distinctions, they were yet ignorant of the rules of heraldry and confused in recent generations their arms. They neglected their old seals and turned to later English dictionaries of heraldry for their bearings and mottoes. They sometimes bore at random the arms of one family of the name or another, and were unconscious of the obligation to prove their hereditary right to their use.

## INTRODUCTION.

The present head of the Carolina family of Lowndes, attracted by the successful investigations of Somerby and Chester, American genealogists long resident in England, and desirous of placing upon permanent record the most serviceable career of his ancestors in the United States, as well as of embodying in correct form as much of the family pedigree as could be authoritatively traced, authorized and approved the memoir contained in the following pages, which was written for the Historical and Genealogical Register, and is found in the number of that periodical for April, 1876.

The portrait, which faces the title page, has been engraved from a photograph of the figure of William Lowndes, as he is represented among a group of members of the House of Representatives in a large picture painted, as is said, by Morse about 1820. The sketches of the heads of those gentlemen whose portraits have thus been preserved were made by the artist from his seat in the gallery of the old chamber of the House, as he looked down upon the floor. Mr. Lowndes never sat for his portrait, and the representation thus disadvantageously taken of him is the only one that can recall, however feebly, his personal appearance.

The Appendix, which has been divided into two parts, will be found to contain in the first part, copies and extracts of those wills and deeds referred to in the narratives which establish the connection between the Cheshire and Carolina families, and in the second, copies of some of the documents in the Record Office at London, which illustrate the connection of the Overton family of Lowndes with the Province of South Carolina, and throw light upon its early settlement and administration.

The writer regrets the imperfections of the accompanying genealogy. The destruction of records and family papers in the Carolinas has been so great, in the confusion of the times, that he has found it a matter of unusual difficulty to determine the facts and dates herein given. The genealogy is not free, as he fears, from omissions, nor, perhaps, from errors. It has been his constant endeavor to be accurate, and he will gladly receive any facts which may illustrate his subject from any who may be able to communicate them.

BOSTON, MAY 1, 1876.

# MEMOIR.

# LOWNDES OF SOUTH CAROLINA.

AMONG the leading families of the State of South Carolina, in by-gone days, there was hardly one that exercised so strong an influence throughout its colonial dependence, and the first half century of its existence as one of the United States, as that of Lowndes of Charleston, and of Colleton County where were its first plantations,—a junior branch of an old and very numerous English family which attained its highest honors in the mother country during the reign of Queen Anne.

For well nigh a century from the year 1725, when Mr. Thomas Lowndes of Overton, in the county of Cheshire, and a descendant of the "*anciente familye* of Lowndes of Legh Hall," was busily engaged in schemes for the settlement of South Carolina, of which he held the patent of Provost Marshal, and was in active correspondence with the Board of Trade, at Whitehall,—down to the period of the Missouri Compromise in 1820, and the lamented death, two years later, of William Lowndes of Charleston, then nominated, after ten years of eminent service in Congress, as a candidate for the Presidency of the United States,—the strenuous character of their race had maintained a continual representation of their name in the service of the colony and state.

When Crowfield, the family residence on the Ashley river, was burned with all its contents, soon after the Revolution, the library, together with its books, portraits and papers, including a pedigree and all the early correspondence with their relatives in England and the West Indies, were utterly destroyed. As the generation then living, according to tradition, were very familiar with the history of their line, and as little importance was then attached to a continuance of that intercourse which had been rudely severed by the outbreak of the War of Independence, no steps were taken to make any record of the history of the Carolina family, and so it happened after the lapse of two generations of planters, who were thoroughly content with their lot in life, and, "*incuriosi suorum*," were unaware of the importance to their descendants of a full family record, that, when there arose among them, a few years since, the natural spirit of inquiry into their antecedents, and a desire to establish anew their traditional connection with England, there was no where in Carolina any paper or record of the family descent, or even of the family correspondence in the last century. Beyond an old seal and a few pieces of English porcelain dinner service sent from England to Rawlins Lowndes, subsequently President of South Carolina, soon after his second marriage in 1750, and decorated with his arms, there was no clue to which branch of the name in England the Carolina planters had been related.

Several years since, Major Rawlins Lowndes, formerly of the Army, and now of Hopeland, near Staatsburgh on Hudson, authorized the inquiry which, conducted by the writer in the West Indies and in England, resulted, after many unforeseen delays, in perfecting anew proofs of that pedigree which had been consumed at the burning of Crowfield nearly a hundred years before.

A comparison of the arms upon the seal and dinner service with that of Lowndes of Bostock House and Hassall Hall, in Burke's History of the Commoners, showed them to be identical, save with the proper difference when borne by a younger son, but the genealogy of the Bostock line, as recorded by Burke, although it showed a representation in the American Colonies at a late period, contained no mention of any possible ancestor of Charles Lowndes of St. Kitts, the founder of the Carolina family.

A correspondence was thereupon instituted with the clergy in the island of St. Christopher, usually called St. Kitts, as it was known from the printed notes of his grandson, the late Hon. Thomas Lowndes, that Mr. Charles Lowndes had come with his family from that island. After an interval of some months, an answer was received from the late Rev. Ebenezer Elliott, then rector of Christ Church, Nicola town, and St. Mary's, Cayou, St. Kitts, giving a record of all births, marriages, and deaths under the Lowndes name before the removal to Carolina. A diligent search was commenced in the record office at London, and a careful examination was made of all the wills which seemed to bear upon the family of either Mr. Thomas Lowndes, of Overton, the first Provost Marshal of

Carolina under the king, or that of the Bostock line. Wills were transcribed, parish registers were searched, and the present representative of the Bostock family in England, now merged in the female line, Miss Sophia Kirkby Reddall, of Congleton, niece and heiress of the last Mr. Lowndes of Hassall, caused an examination of the family papers in her own possession to be made by her solicitor.

It became at length evident, although not till the end of a long and wearisome inquiry, which was carried on at intervals for upwards of five years, that there were material errors and omissions in the English pedigrees, the result of an imperfect and probably hasty examination of the papers of the late Mr. William Lowndes of Hassall, the last representative of his name, before they were submitted to Mr. Burke's compilers for their perusal and use in the preparation of his most comprehensive book, "The History of the Commoners of Great Britain."

As Mr. Thomas Lowndes, Provost Marshal of Carolina in 1725, was of the Overton family, an especial search was also made in the will offices and among the church records of the various parishes in Cheshire where the family name was found, for a proof of his pedigree and with the hope of bringing to light the presumed relationship between this gentleman and Charles Lowndes, whose son Rawlins had, as early as 1741, succeeded to the provost marshalship, with the approval of the assignee of the patent. The wills of all persons recorded under the name of Lowndes at the probate office in Chester were carefully examined, and full extracts were taken from the parish registers of Sandbach, Middlewich and Astbury, but while the family of Mr. Thomas Lowndes of Overton, and afterwards of Westminster — although never himself, after his appointment, in the new world — was clearly ascertained, there was no trace of Charles Lowndes, nor any one of his name.

In the autumn of 1872, the writer, who was then in London, procured some additional lists of wills registered at Doctors' Commons, under the name of Lowndes, with copies of the names of all persons mentioned in them. Among them he read the name of Charles Lowndes as found in the will of Frances Lowndes of Covent Garden. A copy of the will was immediately procured. While it was, at once, evident that, although her name nowhere appeared in the history of the Hassall family, she could have belonged to no other, and that her place in the record could be marked out with absolute precision, it was also apparent that the omission of her name was not the only one of her generation, and that further additions to the family genealogy would probably be found.

In the summer of 1874, by the kindness of Miss Reddall, a copy of the will of William Weld of Weld House and Hassall Hall, who died in 1705, in which the name of Charles Lowndes the elder occurs, was furnished the writer, and from Mr. William H. Turner were received abstracts of certain deeds relative to the Lowndes property at Congleton.*

From these various papers, the following genealogical sketch has been prepared, imperfect as it must always remain from the destruction of so many records in the disorganized condition of South Carolina during the last fifteen years. The genealogy, however, establishes perfectly the connection which was known by tradition to have existed between the old family of Cheshire and the officers of the crown in the province of South Carolina a century and a quarter ago.

WILLIAM[1] LOWNDES,† a descendant of a younger son of the family of Lowndes, of Overton, in Smallwood, and itself a branch of the ancient family of Lowndes of Legh Hall, near Middlewich, bought, in the reign of Queen Elizabeth, Bostock House in Little Hassall, in the parish of Sandbach, all in the county Palatine of Chester, from the family of Bostock of Moreton Say in the county of Salop. He married Ellen, daughter of ——, and had issue:

    i. ELLEN,[2] bapt. Sept. 25, 1580.
    ii. JOAN,[2] bapt. Oct. 21, 1582.
    iii. WILLIAM,[2] bapt. June 9, 1585, who died in childhood.
2.  iv. RICHARD,[2] who succeeded as heir.
    v. THOMAS,[2] bapt. March 15, 1590-1; buried May 8, 1591.

Mr. Lowndes died 4th June, 1590, and by his will, proved 9th October in the same year, appointed his wife, and his brothers Richard and Thomas, executors of his will.

2. RICHARD[2] LOWNDES, gent., of Bostock House, baptized 22d Jan. 1587–8; married 11th Aug. 1611, Elizabeth, daughter of —— Rawlins, and had issue:

    i. MARGERY,[3] bapt. Sept. 17, 1612.
    ii. ELIZABETH,[3] bapt. Oct. 22, 1613.
    iii. RICHARD,[3] bapt. April 19, 1615, who died in infancy.
    iv. ELLEN,[3] bapt. Feb. 27, 1617–18.

By his second wife, Margery, daughter of ——, Mr. Lowndes had one son:—

3. v. JOHN.[3]

---

* By the will of William Weld, his estates passed to his great nephew, Richard Lowndes, of Bostock House and Hassall Hall, son of Richard, and nephew of Charles Lowndes the elder. From the accession of Mr Richard Lowndes to the Hassall property, Bostock House ceased to be the family residence. Ormerod, in his History of Cheshire, thus describes the estates of Bostock and Hassall Hall, as they appeared in 1818.

Of Bostock Hall, he says: "The hall, from which this estate derives its name, is a farm house, containing within its walls some portion of an ancient mansion, which was defended by a moat, of which a part is remaining, and was the property and occasional residence of the Bostocks of Moreton Say, co. Salop. Henry Bostock of that place, by an *Inq. p. m.* 23. Eliz., is found to hold (inter alia) lands in Hassall from the lord of Hulfield, in socage."

"The Hall of Hassall is a very respectable residence, finished with gables, and surrounded with antiquated gardens and offices. The situation is on an elevated knoll, where the neighboring country undulates agreeably, and the circumstances of the term interest of the possessor, "with impeachment of waste," have already ornamented it with pleasure grounds and hedge rows, with trees of growth and proportions strikingly distinguished from those of the adjacent townships."

† Burke's History of the Commoners.

On 4th Jan. 1651, Mrs. Margery Lowndes died, and Mr. Lowndes dying 20th April, 1652, was succeeded by his son,

3. JOHN[3] LOWNDES, gent., of Bostock House, baptized 24th April, 1625. He married Jane, daughter of John Welde, gent., of Weld House, in Newbold Astbury, and co-heir to her brother, William Weld, Esq., of Weld House and Hassall Hall.

By his wife Jane, Mr. Lowndes had ten children:
    i. RICHARD,[4] bapt. at Sandbach, Oct. 13, 1615, who succeeded as heir.
    ii. JOHN,[4] bapt. at Sandbach, Nov. 8, 1646.
    iii. MARY,[4] bapt. at Sandbach, June 4, 1648; m. —— Savyle.
    iv. AUDREY,[4] bapt. at Sandbach, June 5, 1649; m. John Walker.
    v. ELLEN,[4] bapt. at Sandbach, April 19, 1651; m. Robert Bennett.
    vi. CHRISTOPHER,[4] bapt. at Sandbach, Aug. 27, 1652.
    vii. EDWARD,[5] bapt. at Sandbach, Aug. 1, 1653.

Not long after the birth of his seventh child, Mr. Lowndes, as appears by the deeds of Congleton Borough, moved to Middlewich,* where, by an indenture dated 13th Oct. 1657, he made a feoffment to William Welde of Newbold Astbury and John Welde of London of certain premises which he held as heir of his father Richard Lowndes. It is probable that there were born to Mr. Lowndes, while a resident of Middlewich, his younger children, of whose existence the compilers of the family history appear to have been unaware; for, in addition to the children whose baptisms are recorded in the Sandbach records, Mr. Lowndes had:
    viii. FRANCES.[4]
4.  ix. CHARLES,[4] who was bapt. at Middlewich, Dec. 6, 1658, and was described in the parish register as "son of John Lownes."
    x. WILLIAM.[4]

Mr. Lowndes made his will 18th May, 1667, and died the same day. He was buried two days later at Sandbach. His wife, who was co-executrix of his will, died 2d Feb. 1690, and was buried at Worthenbury in Flintshire.

Frances[4] Lowndes, of Covent Garden, made her will 29th March, 1690. She did not long survive, for the will was proved 11th April following. In her will she mentions her mother Jane, her brothers Richard[4] and Charles,[4] her sisters Mary,[4] Audrey[4] and Ellen,[4] and their husbands, who have not, hitherto, been anywhere recorded. She also mentions her sister-in-law Sarah, wife of Charles,[4] and their son Charles,[5] to whom she left a bequest of money which was to be paid him when he attained the age of twenty-one years. She also mentions her cousin, Ann Whittingham, the daughter of her mother's sister, Elizabeth Weld, who had married Thomas Whittingham, gent., of Brereton.

It is worthy of note in this place that the brother of Mrs. Jane Weld Lowndes, William Weld, of Weld House and Hassall Hall, who died at Hassall, and was buried at Sandbach, 23d April, 1705, bequeathed by will to his nephew Charles[4] Lowndes, the elder, an annuity of £5. No trace of

---

  * Middlewich and Sandbach are adjoining parishes, and the Lowndes family which had been settled in the neighborhood from the earliest dates had become wealthy, in the seventeenth century, from their success in the opening of salt mines on their property. Of these mines in Cheshire which have now been worked for several centuries, an English writer (Littell's Living Age, May 2, 1874, No. 1560, p. 349) says, in 1871 an enormous amount of salt was sent out of that country to foreign lands and the home market. "The demand increases, and the supply as yet shows no sign of failure, for the salt district occupies about twenty six square miles, of which not more than five have been hitherto worked. As a single square yard of surface is reckoned to cover one hundred and twenty tons of salt, it will be understood that the total quantity is amazing."

the three younger children of John³ Lowndes had been found by Mr. Burke in the Hassall papers, nor was their existence known to the representatives of the family in England, until the discovery of the existence of Frances⁴ and Charles⁴ had led, at the request of the writer, to a re-examination of the early wills, and the discovery by Miss Reddall in the will of William Weld, of the tenth child, William⁴ Lowndes, of whom, however, we have no other trace.

4. CHARLES⁴ LOWNDES, the elder, as he was known and described in the family papers, married Sarah, daughter of ———, and had one son :
    5. i. CHARLES,⁵ b. ———.

5. CHARLES⁵ LOWNDES, the younger, the ancestor of all of the name of Lowndes in South Carolina, who emigrated in early life to St. Christopher's, or, as it is usually called, St. Kitts, the largest of the Leeward Islands. Soon after his arrival he married Ruth, daughter of Henry Rawlins and ——— his wife.* By this marriage he connected himself with a numerous and influential family, long established in the island, for, as early as 1635, the name of Rawlins is found, and more than once among the list of passengers to St. Kitts from England. Henry Rawlins was in the third generation of planters there, and although he had been at one time a heavy loser by the depredations of the French cruisers, as appears by a record of the year 1705 in the state paper office at London, showing that he had sustained damage on one such occasion, to the amount of £961. 15s. 3d., of which a third part was subsequently recovered, he was enabled to bequeath to his daughter a considerable estate, both real and personal. Mr. Lowndes, whose three children were born to him before the year 1723, embarrassed his property by free living and an unrestrained expenditure, as his grandchildren were informed by their father, and, in 1730, having resigned his position in the Council as representative of the parish of St. Peter, Basseterre, to which he had been elected in the previous year, sailed with his family for Charleston, South Carolina. He was soon after followed by his negroes and movable property, paying £25 duties upon his slaves, and £54. 8s. 8d. on his effects. He executed a mortgage, recorded in the registry of deeds at Charleston, on the 7th of March, 1731, to secure certain bills of exchange drawn by him on the 18th of February previous.†

Mr. Lowndes died in Charleston, March, 1736. His children were:
    6. i. WILLIAM.⁶
    7. ii. CHARLES.⁶
    8. iii. RAWLINS,⁶ b. January, 1721.

6. WILLIAM⁶ LOWNDES, the eldest of these brothers, accompanied his mother on her return to St. Kitts after the death of her husband, whom she survived more than twenty-seven years, dying in Christ Church, Nichola Town, 25th July, 1763. She was buried there on the following day.

---

\* Mr. Elliott was not able to find the record of Mr. Henry Rawlins's marriage. In a lawsuit, instituted in 1716, at St. Kitts, the papers of which are preserved among the colonial records at London, there is a deposition of one Robert Davis, showing that Henry Rawlins and Ruth Garner, widow, had seized a long time before upon land in Basseterre, to which Davis conceived he had a claim, and the deposition recites much of Mr. Rawlins's doings, but says nothing further of the widow Garner. The assumption is reasonable that Mr. Rawlins married the widow, and that Mrs. Charles Lowndes had thus received at baptism the name of Ruth from her mother who bore it.

† Among the acts passed in 1733 by the Colonial Legislature was one entitled, "An act to encourage Charles Lowndes, Esquire, to make a new machine to Pound and Beat Rice and to appropriate the benefit thereof to himself."

William Lowndes was married at Christ Church, April 7th, 1739, to Mary, daughter of Nicholas and Mary Taylor. Their children were:
  i. MARY,[7] bapt. June 1, 1740.
  ii. JOHN-TAYLOR,[7] bapt. Aug. 1, 1744, named in the will of his uncle Charles Lowndes. John-Taylor[7] Lowndes m. ——— and had : —
    i. *John Lowndes*,[8] m. ———, dau. of ——— Bailey of Domenica, and had :
      i. Henrietta,[9] m. Rev. Henry Newman, of Roseau, Domenica.
      ii. Grace,[9] m. ——— Walsh, of Roseau, Domenica, and had issue.

Mr. John[8] Lowndes was Surveyor-general of Dominica. He died in 1812.

7. CHARLES[6] LOWNDES, at the time of his father's death, was about seventeen years of age. His portrait, taken not long before his death, represents a very tall man, with a countenance indicating great determination and fixity of purpose, traits which have been recognized in Carolina as characteristics of the race since Thomas Lowndes, as agent for the duke of Newcastle, had first visited the colony, as early as 1685. Charles[6] Lowndes finished his education under the care of Mr. Robert Hall, a lawyer of position and influence, and soon after established himself as a planter in Colleton County. In 1752, he was appointed Provost Marshal in immediate succession to his brother Rawlins,[6] and held the office several years. He married Sarah, daughter of ——— Parker, and had :
  i. CHARLES,[7] m. Jeannie Perry.*

Mr. Lowndes made his will 18th Jan. 1763, and died the same year. In his will, which was proved in the following May, he mentioned his brother Rawlins,[6] and his nephew John Taylor[7] Lowndes, of St. Kitts, and bequeathed his estate to his wife and son.

8. RAWLINS[6] LOWNDES, who was about fourteen years of age when his mother returned to St. Kitts, had been placed by her in the family of the resident provost marshal, Mr. Robert Hall, as his guardian. This gentleman, who possessed a large library, of which his ward was a diligent student, carefully directed, during the four remaining years of his most useful life, the education of his pupil in the study of the law. Such was the value of Mr. Hall's training, and such was the diligence of young Mr. Lowndes, that on the death of his guardian in January, 1740, it proved to be the well-nigh unanimous desire of the provincial bar that the position of Provost Marshal should be but temporarily filled, and the permanent appointment reserved till he came of age and be enabled to take the oath of office. Early in 1742, Mr. Lowndes received the appointment, which he held for ten years, when he was succeeded, as we have already seen, by his brother Charles.[6]

The office of Provost Marshal corresponded to that of High Sheriff, and had been granted to Mr. Thomas Lowndes, of Westminster, Gent., 27th Sept. 1725. A copy of his Patent, which contains a curious provision, is preserved at the Record Office, London.†

* The authority for this lady's name depends solely upon an old rhyme, for which the neighborhood rather than the family were responsible, handed down through the retentive memory of the late Hon. James L. Petigru:
  "H—ll of a wedding over the Ferry ;
  Charley Lowndes to Jeannie Perry."
The ferry, in the neighborhood of which this old fashioned jollification seems to have taken place, was Parker's Ferry, on the Edisto River.

† Plantations General, vol. 51, p. 63.
"1725, Sept. 27th, Patent for Mr. Tho: Lowndes to be Provost Marshall, Clerk of the Peace and Clerk of the Crown in South Carolina."
"KNOW all Men by these Presents, that We the true and absolute Lords Proprietors of Carolina, do hereby give and grant unto *Thomas Lowndes, Gent.*, his Heirs and Assigns

After Mr. Lowndes retired from office and commenced the active practice of the law, he was elected a member of the Legislature. He carried as zealous a spirit of fidelity to the discharge of his duties into this assembly as he did to the conduct of his cases at the bar. By his untiring industry and impressive speech, no less than by his intellectual power and that spirit of absolute independence by which he was best known among the public men of his time, Mr. Lowndes soon rose to be Speaker of the House. He was also Justice of the Quorum. He discharged upon a writ of *habeas corpus* Powell, a printer of Charleston, who had been imprisoned by the Governor and Council. In 1766, he received from the Crown the appointment of associate judge.

On the 13th of May, 1766, he delivered the first judicial opinion rendered in America upon the Stamp Act, declaring it against common rights and the Constitution, and refusing to enforce it in his court. His rapid success at *nisi prius*, and his superior influence with juries, excited the enmity of Chief Justice Gordon, who laid before the Governor and Council charges of misbehavior against him. He was, however, unanimously acquitted. In 1775, he was removed from the Bench under the prerogative of the Governor, owing to a letter of the Attorney General, Simpson, who was also Secretary to the Governor and Council, and thus in a position to have great influence with them. Simpson, who feared the impending troubles, shortly after returned to England. Mr. Lowndes's reputation as one of the Judges of the Province had, however, become so well known in England, that, on information of his removal by the Colonial Authority, the Home Government appointed Gordon to a situation in Jamaica, and directed the commission of Chief Justice of South Carolina to be issued in favor of Mr. Lowndes.

The Provincial Congress, as it was styled, called in defiance of the royal authority, met on the first of June, 1775. Henry Laurens was chosen President. A Committee of Safety was immediately appointed, which consisted of thirteen members who were vested with supreme power. Of this

the Office and Place, and Offices and Places of *Provost Marshall, Clerk of the Peace*, and *Clerk of the Crown* of and in the Province of South Carolina in America, for the several and respective natural lives of the said Thomas Lowndes and Hugh Watson of the Middle Temple, Gent., to execute the same by the said Thomas Lowndes, his heirs and assigns, or by his or their sufficient Deputy or Deputies. And we do hereby authorize and impower the said Thomas Lowndes, His Heirs and Assigns to demand and receive take and enjoy all Salaries, Wages, Fees, Allowances, Profits, Perquisites, Travelling Charges, Bill Mony, Benefits, Immunities, Privileges, Advantages and Emoluments anywise incident or appertaining to the said Offices or Places or any of them in as ample and beneficial manner as any former Provost Marshall or Marshalls, Clerk of the Peace, and Clerk of the Crown of any other Province or Colony in America, have or hath used, had received or enjoyed. And Lastly We do hereby revoke and make void all former commissions granted for all or any of the said Offices or Places by us or by our Predecessors, or by any Governor or Governors of the said Province of South Carolina. Witness our hands and the seal of the said Province this twenty-seventh Day of September, Anno Domini, 1725.

[Signed]   Beaufort      Jon. Tyrrell
           Craven        Hen. Bertie
           Ja. Bertie    J. Colleton."

This patent was accompanied by the further grant to Thomas Lowndes of four baronies of land in the province, of twelve thousand acres each, by possession of which he became one of the original landgraves of the colony. When the government of Carolina was taken from the Lords Proprietors in 1729, Mr. Lowndes surrendered his patent, and in the following year received a renewal of it from the crown, under date 30th Nov. 1730. Hardly two months later, 11th Feb. 1731, Mr. Lowndes assigned it to George Morley, who soon after left England for Charleston, and assumed the duties of the office. In 1736, Morley returned to England, and on his nomination, Mr. Robert Hall was appointed to succeed him, and held the office, as we have seen, till his death. A temporary appointment was then given by the governor, Colonel Bull, to Mr. William Williamson, who held it till the 1st March, 1742-3, when Rawlins Lowndes received his commission.

committee Mr. Lowndes was chosen the third member, being preceded only by Mr. Laurens and Mr. Charles Pinckney. That he was influential in their debates may be seen in the following letter of Andrew Marvell to William Henry Drayton, written at

"Charleston, Sunday, August 12th, 1775.

"I have twice pushed hard for the 'Resolution for attaching Estates in case of Desertion,' but have not been lucky enough to get a second. The matter, however, is not *rejected*, only postponed. Rawlins postponator declares the resolution not proper to proceed from the Committee of South Carolina, and so arbitrary, that nothing but the Divan of Constantinople could think of promulgating such a law."

He opposed the pretensions of the British Government, as violations of the rights of English subjects, and he was the first to denounce on the floor of the House the claim of taxation without parliamentary representation as the chief grievance of all. Yet, while there were none in their attitude more bold than he in Carolina, he did not till the last abandon the hope of reconciliation with England. Either from his training as a lawyer, his position as a judge, and his peculiar means of ascertaining the temper of the friends of the Colonies in England, he had been led, as he stated later in life, to the belief that the early measures of hostility would lead to reconciliation and to the retirement of the British Ministry from their unfortunate position on colonial questions.

His opposition to all harsh acts at this time and to the declaration of independence in the Colony was consistent with his uniform policy to oppose all measures that would tend to close the door to reconciliation, while there was yet a hope of success. A fortnight later, the last Royal Governor, Lord William Campbell, arrived to supersede Colonel William Bull. The Provincial Congress made him an address which he refused to receive, as he did to recognize their existence. On the 16th of the following September, he fled to the British ship-of-war Tamar, carrying the great seal of the Colony. Six months later, on the twenty-fourth of March, 1776, South Carolina declared her independence of the British Crown, and Mr. Rutledge was elected President of the State. Mr. Lowndes, who had been one of the committee of eleven to devise a plan of government, was chosen a member of the legislative council.

On the 10th of March, 1778, he succeeded to the Presidency of South Carolina, and was so formally proclaimed at the State House on that day, "under the discharge of the Artillery both from the Troops and Forts and the discharge of small arms."* He gave his approval to the Constitution of 1778, by which the power to reject a legislative act, the *veto* power, which had been vested in the Executive, was relinquished, and a subject of earnest contention in the State, since John Rutledge had rejected the first bill for a reformed constitution, was thus settled in favor of the representatives of the people.

After the treaty of alliance between France and the United States had been concluded, the British Government sent the Earl of Carlisle, Governor Johnstone, and Mr. Eden† to America, as commissioners authorized to offer

---
* Letter of James Cannon to the Honorable George Boyle, Vice-President of the Commonwealth of Pennsylvania, 14th March, 1778.
† Ramsay, i. p. 293.

Congress a repeal of all those Acts of the Crown which had led the Colonies to declare their independence, and to threaten with the extreme penalties of war all those who should continue to prefer an alliance with France to a re-union with the mother country. The Commissioners, repelled by Congress, determined to address the people of each state, and sent a vessel under a flag into the port of Charleston, with their propositions separately addressed to the governor, the assembly, the military, the clergy, and the people of South Carolina. By order of President Lowndes, the vessel was detained in the roadstead, below the harbor, until the council was convened, and the chief men of each class of the people to whom these propositions were addressed, were assembled. When the letter of the Commissioners had been opened and read, a resolution was drawn up and unanimously voted requiring the flag-ship to immediately leave the waters of the State. President Lowndes accompanied the resolution with a stern reprimand of the attempt to violate the constitution of the country, by the offer to negotiate with the state in its separate capacity.

As soon as it was known, towards the end of the year 1778, that the British authorities intended to transfer the seat of active hostilities to the southern states, President Lowndes laid a general embargo, and prohibited the sailing of vessels from any port of the State.* He ordered all live stock from the islands and exposed parts of the coast to be transported inland, and sent an address to the Legislature calling upon them to take the most energetic measures for successful resistance. In that message, he said, "Our inveterate and obdurate enemy, foiled in the northern states, and by the valor and good conduct of the inhabitants compelled to abandon their hope of conquest there, have turned their arms more immediately against the southern states, in hopes of better success. They are now in possession of Savannah, the capital of Georgia, from whence, if not prevented, an easy transition may be made into this country. This situation of danger, gentlemen, calls for your most serious consideration. Our whole force and strength should be exerted to stop the progress of the enemy."

President Lowndes gave to General Lincoln, who had been sent by Congress from the North to the command of the southern department, an earnest support, and exerted his official and private influence in vigilant and unremitted efforts for the defence of Charleston.

In 1779, Mr. Lowndes was succeeded in the Presidency by John Rutledge. He shared, however, in the defence of Charleston, and was personally a heavy sufferer by the enemy's depredations along the coast and rivers, as he was obliged on one occasion to drive into Charleston, in his carriage hauled by a yoke of oxen, his horses having all been carried off by a sudden raid.

On his retirement from the Presidency, he had been elected a member of the Senate from St. Bartholomew's, the parish he had before represented in the other House. Upon the declaration of peace, he was chosen to the Legislature as Representative from Charleston, and was continued in this position by reëlection until the removal of the seat of government to Columbia led him to decline further service.

The constitution of the United States, recommended by the general convention at Philadelphia, in 1787, was received by the legislature of South Carolina, and read before the House of Representatives on the 16th of January, 1788. It was debated for three days in Committee of the Whole—

* Ramsay, i. p 296.

by Charles Pinckney, Gen. Charles Cotesworth Pinckney, John Rutledge, and Pierce Butler, who had been delegates to the Federal Convention,— by the Speaker, John Julius Pringle, by Robert Barnwell, Edward Rutledge, Dr. David Ramsay the historian, all men of signal ability, the reputation of whose talents has long survived them, and all in favor of the constitution, and by Rawlins Lowndes alone on behalf the minority in opposition to it.[*]

Among the discussions upon the adoption of the Constitution there is no debate more able, nor, in the light of history since, is there one more curious and interesting. Mr. Lowndes, who spoke four times, objected principally to the restrictions upon slavery, nor did he shrink as others did from saying so,—to the provisions which gave Congress power to regulate commerce, and to the centralization of power in the Federal Government. He concluded on the third day in these words:

"I desire to thank the House for their very great indulgence in permitting me, on behalf of those members who have desired that I should fully express my sentiments, to debate it at such length. The vast importance of the subject will plead my excuse. I thank the gentlemen on the other side of the question for the candid and fair manner in which they have answered my arguments. Popularity is what I have never courted, but, on this issue, I have spoken merely to point out those dangers to which my fellow citizens are exposed, dangers so evident, that, when I cease to exist, I wish for no other epitaph than to have inscribed on my tomb, 'Here lies the man who opposed the Constitution, because it was ruinous to the liberty of America.'"

When the question on the assembly of the convention to consider the Constitution was about to be put, Colonel James Mason, of Little River, by desire of the minority members of the House, rose and formally thanked Mr. Lowndes for his opposition.

The Convention assembled on the 12th of May. Mr. Charles Pinckney opened the debate on the 14th, and on the 23d the Constitution was adopted by a vote of one hundred and forty members in its favor, to seventy-three in opposition.

The debate in convention, however, attracted but little notice in the State, so thoroughly had the battle been fought in the legislature. The opponents of the Federal Constitution had lost by the refusal of Mr. Lowndes to stand for St. Bartholemews the leader of their party, nor could they furnish another to give dignity and interest to debate by a forcible presentation of such objections as had occurred to the ingenious and able reasoning of Mr. Lowndes.

Many years ago, one who remembered him well, contributed to a Southern journal his impressions of Mr. Lowndes's character and attainments to this effect.

Possessed of a strong judgment, a clear, logical, and discriminating mind, he enforced his opinions, unmindful of their popularity, with strength and freedom. In a debate, at Charleston, when the question of the right of his constituents to instruct their representatives was under discussion in the House, he opposed it with vehemence and great force, declaring it to be a pretension which required representatives to suppress their own judgment and substitute that of others, and which renders their oath to discharge their duty according to their best judgment, a mere form and in effect a sham.

Mr. Lowndes married, 15th of August, 1748, Amarinthia, daughter of Thomas Elliott, of Rantoules, Stone River. Mrs. Lowndes died 14th of

[*] Elliot's Debates, vol. iv. pp. 253-316.

January, 1750, and was buried by the side of her parents at the cemetery near Rantoules.

Mr. Lowndes married, 2nd, December 23d. 1751, Mary, daughter of —— Cartwright, of Charleston. By this lady he had:

    i.   AMARINTHIA,[7] b. July 29, 1754; m. Sept. 23, 1776, Roger Parker Sanders, Esq., and after his death, married, second, —— Champney, Esq.
    ii.  MARY,[7] b. Aug. 1755; d. unm.
    iii. RAWLINS,[7] b. November 5, 1757; d. in childhood.
    iv.  HARRIET,[7] m. —— Brown, and had:
        i. LOWNDES,[9] who m. Margaretta Livingston, dau. of Hon. John R. Livingston, third son of Judge Robert R. Livingston, of New-York. By this marriage Mr. Lowndes Brown had:
            i. *Harriet-Lowndes*,[9] who m. August, 1855, Henry, Baron Solwyns, of the Belgian Diplomatic Service.
    v.   SARAH-RUTH,[7] b. 1764; m. —— Simmons; d. 1852.
9. vi.  THOMAS,[7] b. January 22, 1766.
10. vii. JAMES,[7] b. ——, 1769.

Mr. Lowndes married, third, Sarah, daughter of —— Jones, of Georgia, and had:

11. viii. WILLIAM[7]-JONES, b. Feb. 1782.

By his success at the bar and by fortunate investments in land Mr. Lowndes left to his children large estates on the Ashley, Combahee, and Santee Rivers. He died in Charleston, 24 August, 1800, and was buried in St. Philip's Church. A few months later, his widow, while driving with her son, was thrown from a chaise and instantly killed.

9. THOMAS[7] LOWNDES was educated in the city of Charleston, and at the family residence on the Ashley River.

A child of seven years at the outbreak of the Revolution, he was old enough to fix in his memory as they occurred the entire succession of events which led the colonies from unheeded petitions for redress to their Declaration of Independence, and through a weary and painful war to an absolute union of independent States. He was already of age when he studied, as part of his preparation for the practice of law, those debates upon the new Constitution he may have heard in the old State House at Charleston, where his father had stood as the solitary speaker in opposition to an able and triumphant majority. Inheriting strong powers of mind, he cultivated in his youth that taste for English literature and the study of constitutional law, which has always largely characterized the best minds in the Southern States. Remaining unmarried till, for those days, the somewhat ripe age of thirty-two, he met as guests at his father's table in town and country a long succession of men from the North and the South who had made their names illustrious in the public service, either in peace or war. He had been, too, an attentive listener to their interesting discussions upon the questions how best to build up a free Republic in the new world. He was thus by study, by acquaintance and by family tradition, no less than by the almost inevitable tendencies of the profession he had chosen as the recognized path to public life, a politician, familiar with the whole subject of national legislation,—like so many other leaders of opinion under the old order of things in the Carolinas,—and he fitted himself with care for his turn of duty, when the time determined in his own mind should come.

In the autumn of 1800, a few months after his father's death, having already served in the Legislature of the State, he accepted from the Federal party the nomination of Representative from the Charleston District to the Seventh Congress. He took his seat at the opening of the first session on the 7th of December, 1801. On the next day he was appointed to the Committee of Commerce and Manufactures, and was prominent from that time in the discussions of the House. As early as Dec. 14th, almost in the first week of business, he spoke upon the resolution of inquiry into the conduct of Mr. Pickering when Secretary of State, and he took part in "an animated debate,"—as the National Intelligencer of that day, more mindful for the dignity of Congress than are the public journals of our own time, described in language somewhat euphuistic a stormy scene, so often repeated afterwards on any sectional issue,—which occurred over an amendment to the Apportionment Bill providing that Maryland should be entitled to nine rather than eight representatives. The Intelligencer tells us that "a debate of the utmost dilatoriness took place. Much personal recrimination, chiefly on the charge of delay on the one side and precipitation on the other, was exchanged, which we think it our duty entirely to suppress."

Mr. Lowndes on the 15th of March, 1802. opened the debate on the French Spoliation Claims, speaking in favor of their recognition, and urging prompt measures for their settlement. Little could he, or any statesman of that day, foresee the uncertainties of legislation which the history of this measure was in itself to illustrate. Reported formally to Congress again and again by Committees, it finally passed both Houses only to become void by the refusal of the Executive's approval. Again revived and apparently not yet despaired of, these claims, now as old as the century, have already outlived three generations of public men. At the end of the long debate, in April, 1802. in the Act providing for the redemption of the entire public debt of the United States, Mr. Lowndes was in the minority of nineteen members, all federals, who voted against the bill.*

Constant in attendance upon the House, he was earnest and assiduous in committee, and though mingling often in debate, he was yet able to contribute to the discussion something of value in fact and much of weight in judgment, enforced as his sentiments always were by a natural eloquence, which had been carefully cultivated under the sound opinions then entertained by all educated men, who valued the study of oratory not as that of a graceful accomplishment, but as the mastery of an essential influence and tested power over the emotions and conduct of men.

In the intervals between the sessions, Mr. Lowndes, accompanied by his family, visited the Northern States, and passed the summer in New England and the neighborhood of Boston. He was warmly welcomed by his political associates, and received much hospitality from them. An intimate acquaintance with many northern families was thus established, which was maintained with unvarying cordiality through life, and descended to his children.

He resumed his seat at the Second Session, on the 13th of December, 1802. On the 22d of that month, he spoke in the discussion on the circulation of gold coin, which, owing to the erroneous valuation put by the statute upon the eagles and half eagles previously coined, below their metallic worth, had led to their being everywhere hoarded. In the long debate on the 6th of January, 1803, on the cession by Spain of Louisiana to France, he was early upon the floor, urging with force the proposed call upon the Executive for the precise facts of the transaction which had been withheld from Congress.

* National Intelligencer, 14th April, 1802.

Mr. Lowndes was re-chosen to the Eighth Congress, and took his seat in the House on the 29th of October, 1803. He spoke, on the 6th and 8th of the following December, on the constitutional amendment relative to the method of election of President and Vice-President, in favor of postponement till after the ensuing election, and again on the 6th of January, 1804, in opposition to the proposed impeachment of Samuel Chase, a Justice of the Supreme Court, who was tried a few months later by the Senate, and acquitted.

At their session of this year, the Legislature of South Carolina had passed an act repealing all restrictions upon the importation of slaves. The subject early attracted the attention of Congress, and on Tuesday, 14th of February, as will be seen from the following extract from the debates, the following motion by Mr. Bard, of Pennsylvania, was taken into consideration in Committee of the Whole.

" Resolved, that a tax of ten dollars be imposed upon every slave imported into any part of the United States."

On motion of Mr. Jackson, it was agreed to add after the words United States, "or their territories."

MR. LOWNDES. " I will trespass a very short time upon the attention of the House at this stage of the business, but as I have objections to the resolution, it may be proper that I should state them now. I will do so briefly, reserving to myself the privilege of giving my opinion more at length when the bill is before the House, should the resolution be adopted, and a bill brought in. I am sorry, Mr. Speaker, to find that the conduct of the Legislature of South Carolina, in repealing its law prohibitory of the importation of negroes, has excited so much dissatisfaction and resentment as I find it has done with the greater part of this House. If gentlemen will take a dispassionate review of the circumstances under which the repeal was made, I think this dissatisfaction and resentment will be removed, and I should indulge the hope that this contemplated tax will not be imposed. Antecedent to the adoption of the constitution under which we now act, the Legislature of South Carolina passed an act prohibiting the importation of negroes from Africa, and sanctioned it by severe penalties,—I speak from recollection, but I believe not less than the forfeiture of the negro and a fine of one hundred pounds sterling for each brought into the State. This act has been in force until it was repealed by the Legislature at their last session. \* \* \* \* \*

" The law was completely evaded, and for the last year or two, Africans were introduced into the country in numbers little short, I believe, of what they would have been had the trade been a legal one. Under the circumstances, Sir, it appears to me to have been the duty of the Legislature to repeal the law, and remove from the eyes of the people the spectacle of its authority daily violated.

" I beg, Sir, that from what I have said, it may not be inferred that I am friendly to a continuation of the slave trade. I wish the time had arrived when Congress could legislate conclusively upon the subject. I should then have the satisfaction of uniting with the gentleman from Pennsylvania who moved the resolution. Whenever it does arrive, should I then have a seat in this House, I assure him I will cordially support him in obtaining his object. But, Mr. Speaker, I cannot vote for this resolution, because I am sure it is not calculated to promote the object which it has in view. I am convinced that the tax of ten dollars will not prevent the introduction into the country of a single slave. * * * * The gentleman from Pennsylvania, and those who think with him, ought, above all others, to deprecate the passing of this resolution. It appears to me to be directly calculated to defeat their own object,—to give to what they wish to discountenance a legislative sanction, and, further, an interest to the government to permit this trade after it might constitutionally terminate it. When I say that I am myself unfriendly to it, I do not wish, Mr. Speaker, to be misunderstood; I do not mean to convey the idea that the people of the Southern States are universally opposed to it—I know the fact to be otherwise. Many of the people in the Southern States feel an interest in it, and will yield it with reluctance. Their interest will be strengthened by the immense accession of territory to the United States by the cession of Louisiana. * * * * * *

"My greatest objection to this tax is, Mr. Speaker, that it will fall exclusively upon the agriculture of the State of which I am one of the Representatives. However odious it may be to some gentlemen, and however desirous they may be of discountenancing it, I think it must be evident that this tax will not effect their object; that it will not be a discouragement to the trade, nor will the introduction of a single African into the country be prevented. The only result will be that it will produce a revenue to the government. I trust that no gentleman is desirous of establishing this tax with a view to revenue. The State of South Carolina contributes as largely to the revenue of the United States, for its population and wealth, as any state in the Union. To impose a tax falling exclusively on her agriculture would be the height of injustice, and I hope that the Representatives of the landed interest of the nation will resist every measure, however general in its appearance, a tendency of which is to lay a partial and unequal tax upon agriculture."

Mr. BEDINGER. "The gentleman from South Carolina has so fully expressed the opinions I entertain, I shall say but little. Every one who knows my opinions on slavery, may think it strange that I shall give my vote against the resolution. There is no member on this floor more inimical to slavery than I am, yet I am of opinion that the effect of the present resolution, if adopted, will be injurious. I shall, therefore, vote against it."

When on Friday, February 17th, the third day of the debate, the House resumed the discussion of the bill. Mr. Lowndes rose, and after a rapid review of the subject, moved that its further consideration be postponed till the following December. By an amendment, the bill was set down for the second Monday in March, and thus the same end was accomplished, as the House did not sit on that day.

Upon the issue of this debate, Mr. Benton* remarks, "To prevent an erroneous impression being made upon the public by the above proceedings, it is proper to remark, that, during the whole discussion, not a single voice was raised in defence of the act of the Legislature of South Carolina, allowing the importation of slaves, but that, on the contrary, while by some of the speakers its immorality and impolicy were severely censured, by all its existence was deprecated. A large number of those who voted for the postponement, advocated it on the express and sole ground that it would give the Legislature of South Carolina an opportunity, which they believed would be embraced, to repeal the Act."

* Abridgment of Debates, iii. p. 142.

Just three years later, the question was definitely settled by Congress. On the 13th of February, 1807, the House passed the Senate bill, prohibiting the importation of slaves by a vote of one hundred and thirteen members in favor over five in opposition,—and this slender, indeed nominal, minority were members from both free and slave states, who dissented only upon matters of detail, so that, as Mr. Benton observes,[*] "the prohibition of the trade may be deemed unanimous."

Mr. Lowndes passed the summer at the North and in the neighborhood of Philadelphia. He did not reach Washington till the 6th of November following, after the second session of Congress had commenced, and had thus not been in his place when the Committees of the House were appointed; but, a fortnight later, on the announcement of the resignation of Mr. Samuel L. Mitchell, chairman of the Committee on Commerce, who had been appointed by the Legislature of New York a Senator of the United States, it was *Ordered*, "That Mr. Lowndes be appointed chairman of the Committee of Commerce and Manufactures," &c. &c. He thus returned to his old place on the Committee to which he had been first appointed on his entry to the House.

He spoke for the last time in Congress, on the 13th of December, against a bill to regulate and permit the clearance of private armed vessels. His speech, though brief, was marked by the same quick, ready and logical reasoning which had always characterized his appearance in debate. He left Washington on the 6th of March, 1805, and, failing to obtain his reëlection to Congress on the general overthrow of the Federal party in the South, retired to private life. He continued, however, a steadfast adherent to the principles of his party, and earnestly supported John Quincy Adams, when nominated for the presidency against Andrew Jackson. He often remarked, in allusion to the brilliant political career of his brother, William Lowndes, that coming as a Republican later into public life than himself, his brother differed from him in no essential principle of his political faith.

Mr. Lowndes never resumed the practice of the law. He devoted the remainder of his days to the education of his family, and care of his large estates, and especially the cultivation of his plantation Oakland, on the Combahee river. He passed a portion of each year at his residence in Charleston. He entertained both in town and country, with the cordial hospitality characteristic of the manners of the period, and his conspicuous social station. His house was the resort, as his father's had been before him, of distinguished citizens of the State. An occasional journey to the North, where two of his children had married, enabled him to continue those friendships which he had formed when in the public service.

Mr. Lowndes married, on the 8th of March, 1798, Sarah Bond, daughter of Richard Ion, Esquire, of Springfield, St. James, Santee.

By this lady, who united great charm of manner to a handsome and distinguished presence, and whose portrait by Gilbert Stuart has been ranked among the most successful of all his pictures of women, as it was the favorite of the artist himself, Mr. Lowndes had:

 i. RAWLINS,[8] b. May 23, 1789; d. October, 1800.
 ii. MARY-ION,[8] b. August 1, 1800; m. March 12, 1816, to Frederic Kinloch, of Charleston, and had issue:

---

[*] Abridgment of Debates, iii. p. 519.

                i. MARTHA-RUTLEDGE,⁹ b. April 28, 1818: m. Matthew Singleton.
                ii. THOMAS-LOWNDES,⁹ b. January 3, 1820; d. unm.
                iii. CLELAND,⁹ b. October 6, 1823; d. ——, —.
12. iii. RAWLINS,⁸ b. September 1, 1801.
13. iv. THOMAS,⁸ b. June 26, 1803, at New-Haven, Conn.
    v. JACOB-ION,⁸ b. Sept. 19, 1804, at Philadelphia; d. February 7, 1829, unm.
14. vi. WILLIAM-PRICE,⁸ b. Sept. 21, 1806.
15. vii. CHARLES-TIDYMAN,⁸ b. June 28, 1808.
    viii. EDWARD-TILGHMAN,⁸ b. January 15, 1810; d. July, 1837, and was buried in Georgetown, South Carolina.
    ix. HARRIETT,⁸ b. January 18, 1812; m. February 3, 1831, the Hon. William Aiken, proprietor of Jehossee Island, Governor of South Carolina 1844–46, a member of Congress from 1851 to 1857, and has:
                i. HENRIETTA,⁹ who m. Burnett Rhett, Esq., and has issue.
    x. CAROLINE-HUGER,⁸ b. Sept. 25, 1813; d. Sept. 8, 1817.
16. xi. RICHARD-HENRY,⁸ b. March 4, 1815.

Mr. Lowndes died in Charleston, on the 8th July, 1843. He had survived his wife less than three years, as Mrs. Lowndes had died 7th October, 1840.

10. JAMES⁷ LOWNDES, m. Catherine Osborne, and by her had issue:

    i. THOMAS-OSBORNE,⁸ b. 1801; m. 1824, Elizabeth-Wragg, dau. of William-Loughton Smith.
    ii. AMARINTHIA,⁸ b. 1803; m. 1831, Lewis Morris, and had:
        i. ELIZABETH,⁹ died unm.
        ii. LEWIS.⁹
            Mrs. Morris died 1843.
    iii. JAMES,⁸ b. 1806; d. unm. 1838.
17. iv. EDWARD-RUTLEDGE,⁸ b. 1809.
    v. JULIA,⁸ b. 1811; m. 1830, W. Brisbane, and had:
        i. MARY,⁹ m. ——— Hickok.
        ii. JULIA,⁹ m. R. Rhett.
        iii. RUTH,⁹ m. Colden Tracy.
        iv. CATHERINE-OSBORNE,⁹ m. Charles Davis.
        v. AMARINTHIA.⁹
        vi. WILLIAM.⁹
        vii. JAMES.⁹
            Mrs. Brisbane died 1847.
    vi. WILLIAM,⁸ b. 1817; m. 1841, Mary Middleton, and had issue:
        i. HARRIET-KINLOCH.⁹
        ii. MARY-AMARINTHIA.⁹
            Mr. Lowndes died 1865.

Mr. Lowndes died 1839.

11. WILLIAM⁷ LOWNDES, as he is usually styled, since he never used his second baptismal name, was taken by his mother, in his seventh year, to England, and placed at the school of Mr. John Savage, at Brompton Grove. The first glimpse of him in England, is obtained in a letter from Mr. Savage to Mr. Rawlins Lowndes, at Charleston, written in the month of December, 1790. The son's progress was spoken of in cordial approval, and as equal to his father's anticipations. This favorite report was, unhappily, soon followed by one of a different nature, which carried the news of a singular and most unfortunate occurrence to the little boy. After a fatiguing game with his playmates, one day during the heavy snows of the winter of 1791, he sat down to rest by a drift of snow and soon fell fast asleep. He was there left unnoticed by his companions, and was not thought of by them till his unexplained absence, on their return to school, caused a search to be made

for him. He was brought back alive, yet so thoroughly benumbed with cold, that, despite the remedies which were at once given to him, he only escaped with life after a long and severe attack of inflammatory rheumatism. His health, on convalescence, was found to be so seriously affected, that a return to his home and the warm climate of Carolina was pronounced necessary by the physician of the school. Nor was this opinion ill founded, for, during the remainder of his boyhood, cut off from its sports, he struggled against a constitution permanently impaired.

On his return home, he was sent to a school in Charleston, long famous in the South,—the joint establishment of three divines—Dr. Simon Felix Gallagher, a Roman Catholic, Dr. Beust, a Presbyterian, and Dr. Purcell, an Episcopalian. Dr. Gallagher was a man of great ability and learning, and young Lowndes soon showed how quick, capacious, and retentive was his mind. His memory was such that he could repeat long passages of poetry after a single reading. His progress in his studies was most rapid, and seemed to his schoolmates, as they were wont to say in after life, and in warm remembrance of him, absolutely marvellous.* He remained under Dr. Gallagher's charge more than five years, when the teacher at length said of his pupil, that "his mind had drank up knowledge as the dry earth did the rain from heaven,—that he had learned all that his teacher could impart to him, and that he must thenceforth depend on his own guidance for further progress." The pupil was but fifteen. He joined at this time a youth's debating society, and was soon conspicuous for his fluency and readiness in debate. It was remembered of him, afterward, that all his written essays, while at school, had been deemed by the instructors remarkable for their merit. He had, too, some talent for versification, and translated the Odes of Horace into English verse.

His father watched with pride the rapid progress of this child of his old age. Guided by him, the son pursued his studies from an early period, to fit himself for a political career; yet his peculiar desire for information, based, perhaps insensibly, upon an instinctive confidence in his own large capacity for knowledge, seems to have led him into wider paths of learning than were usually entered by those who aspired to political distinction. He had studied the writings of La Place as they appeared, and had attained sufficient proficiency in Greek to correspond years afterwards upon the principles of its pronunciation. He continued to read, under the influence and suggestion of Dr. Gallagher, until he entered the law office of De Saussure, at a later period Chancellor of the State.

Mr. Lowndes was, at this time, conspicuous in society, fond of gaiety, and had some tastes unusual in one of his studious mind. He was fond of horses, and eager in his desire to improve the breed in Carolina. He had, too, a strong infusion of military zeal, and, a few years later, on the formation of the Washington Light Infantry was chosen its first commander.† He was fairly entitled to the distinction; he was head and shoulders taller than his men. At the time of his marriage to Miss Pinckney in 1804, he was hardly more than twenty years of age. As soon as he felt able to practise, he was admitted to the Charleston Bar. He applied to Mr. Cogdell, then City Attorney, for permission to enter his office and assist him, without recom-

---

* Mr. Fraser to Mr. Ravenel.
† This company still exists, and enjoys a conspicuous and honorable position among the widely known militia organizations of the Union. Its visit to Boston at the celebration of the 17th of June, 1875, was a distinct feature in the occurrences of that day.

pense, in its duties.* This proposal was generously refused by Mr. Cogdell, who offered him in turn a partnership on equal terms. The offer was accepted, and in March, 1804, the two gentlemen commenced practice together as law partners. The firm, however, did not continue long, for at the end of the following September, a severe storm raged over the whole of the lower country, and did much damage to the plantations, especially to the rice harvest. When Mr. Lowndes learned that his own valuable plantation had been well nigh ruined by the rains and winds, he felt obliged to go to it at once and direct in person the slow work of restoration. In taking leave of his partner, he modestly regretted that he had been of so little service to him.

As he had never intended to pursue the practice of law as his profession in life, but rather to acquire the power to use it as a means to an end in the work of sound legislation, so he never returned to it. As early as 1806 he was engaged in the discussion of a subject, connected with international law, which bore directly upon the political questions of the day. England was then at war with France and her tributary states, and she had sought help in the great struggle by a grave violation of neutral rights. Her merchants, who had seen with alarm that the maritime trade of Europe was bestowing immense profits upon the commerce of America, made bitter and indignant complaint to Pitt. He speedily determined that neutral trade should cease. An interdict, by the issue of new orders in council, was put upon it, and American vessels with their cargoes were seized and confiscated. To support its action, the British ministry called at this time into its service able pamphleteers, and, among their productions, there was one of great influence and power, which attained a wide circulation, entitled "War in Disguise." It was ascribed at first by some to Canning, by others to James Stephens, a lawyer of great ability, who was, in fact, its author. It was an ingenious and eloquent attempt to show that neutral trade was in effect the maintenance of war against England, and of all the political productions of the time was the best designed and fitted to make quick mischief between two countries peopled by the same race. The claims of England were discussed by Mr. Lowndes in a series of thirteen papers, which appeared in the Charleston Courier over the signature of "A Planter," in the spring and summer of 1806. They were written with great clearness of language and force of reasoning; considered as the production of a very young man, they were not unworthy of the author's later high reputation. They indicated the tendency of his mind to political discussion, and, in a larger view, the turn of thought and sentiment which was nerving the South to overcome all resistance to a declaration of war with England. These papers procured for their writer an election to the general assembly of the State from the Parish of St. Bartholomews' in the autumn of 1806.

Mr. Lowndes began his political career under some light shadows of annoyance in social life, for he supported, with a few other young men of his class, the Republican Party and the political principles of Jefferson. The old Federal leaders of the day were the recognized heads of society, and they resented the defection of their juniors as a revolt from sound principles and just authority. Every social influence was brought to bear upon young men of such striking promise as William Lowndes, Langdon Cheves and Joseph Allston, and compel their return to the Federal fold. Deaf to the

---

* E. S. Thomas, "Reminiscences of sixty-five years," i. p. 104.

persuasion of their elders, these young gentlemen soon found that the principles they openly avowed caused them to be looked upon with aversion and distrust by the Federal authorities, and shut them out from much of the gaiety of town and country life. It was during the service of Mr. Lowndes in the Legislature, from 1806 to 1810, that the change was made in the basis of representation in the State, which lasted down to the abolition of slavery.

The constitutions of 1776 and 1778 had apportioned the representation arbitrarily, and upon the basis of wealth alone. As the upper country increased in population, a change became necessary, and, in 1809, the Legislature passed an act, providing that one half of the members of the lower house should be elected on the basis of population, and the other half on the basis of wealth.

The history of all measures of political reform has shown how difficult it is to take the first steps, and how easy the solution of the riddle afterwards appears when the details of the question have been matured, and its various issues turned into one comprehensive measure. It then becomes a matter of some interest to know who was the author of the system of representation which served its purpose so well in South Carolina for more than fifty years, and secured her, by the ability and character of her congressional reputation, and the honest and dignified administration of her domestic concerns, so great an influence among her sister states. The authorship of the amendment has been attributed by some to Col. Blanding, and by others to Mr. Lowndes. Both were on the committee who reported it, but the original manuscript, interlined and corrected, was in the hand-writing of Mr. Lowndes.*

The political nominations of 1810 were canvassed with an especial reference to the attitude of candidates upon the all important question of the apprehended war with Great Britain. Mr. Lowndes's views were already well known from his letters to the Charleston Courier in 1806. He had no confidence in the shifts and expedients, the Embargo and Non-intercourse Acts of a former administration. He regarded them rather as the illusory schemes of a philosopher, than as the measures of a clearsighted statesman. The commerce they were created to defend, they tended in reality to destroy. The encroachments of England on Neutral Rights had continued in face of such enactments to increase, and had culminated at last on the attack of a British man-of-war on an American frigate in our own waters, in the summer of 1807.

* The late Mr. Francis J. Grayson made the question of the authorship of this amendment a subject of careful study, and wrote upon it an elaborate note, in which he reviewed the various arguments from time to time put forth in Carolina on behalf of the friends of Mr. Lowndes and Col. Blanding. His conclusions were wholly in favor of the claims of the former, and one of his reasons is so entirely in accordance with the conditions of the measure at the time it was under debate, previous to its passage, as to deserve great weight.

Mr. Grayson was of opinion, that there was at that time a desire that Col. Blanding should be regarded as the head of the movement. It was important to conciliate the upper and middle country. It conduced "to this end that the measure should have the approbation of a judicious member from that quarter. Colonel Blanding was the man, less connected than any other with the conflicting parties of the State and commanding the confidence of all. He was willing to lend his aid to the proposed change, was put forward for that end, and gave his help in a mode that necessarily connected his name with it before the people."

The reason here given is one that in its very nature would have occasioned great reserve on the part of Mr. Lowndes and his friends, and such as would prevent not only any recognition of his connection with the movement, but would even lead its friends to obtain the leadership of one who represented as distinctively, as did Col. Blanding, the other sections of the state. Yet it was due to Mr. Lowndes and to his subsequent distinguished reputation that the evidence of his claims should be preserved, and the declaration of Judge Huger, his colleague in the Legislature, who spoke from personal knowledge, and declared to Mr. Grayson that Lowndes and not Blanding was the author, be authoritatively noted as it fell from his lips.

The pride of the American people had been then touched to the quick. In vain had Mr. Canning offered instant and ample apologies,—for it had been every where felt among the young, the bold, and the aspiring, that the very fact that such an occasion for apology should exist was in itself a disgrace. It was in this condition of the Southern mind that Mr. Lowndes received the nomination of the Republicans of the Beaufort and Colleton District, as Representative to the Twelfth Congress. He was elected in 1810, and took his seat in obedience to the executive proclamation, in the early assembly of the House, on the 4th of November, 1811. South Carolina has neither before nor since introduced to the national service three such able men as William Lowndes, John C. Calhoun, and Langdon Cheves, whom she sent to Washington at this time—as new and untried members.

It was not in the nature of Mr. Lowndes to rush into the arena of debate with that eager haste for distinction, so often seen, since it is so natural to men of an acquired local reputation. He was master of himself and felt he could bide the worthy subject and the proper time. He had been named by the Speaker, Mr. Clay, second on the Committee of Commerce and Manufactures, a position which at once gave him influence in those days in shaping the business of the session. He was earnest and diligent in the advancement of all the measures of preparation for war, and made his first speech, 4th of January, 1812, in the support of the bill to provide an additional military force, by an addition to the army of twenty thousand men, and he immediately followed it with another in support of an increase of the naval establishment, voting on this question, during the long debate upon it, for every amendment in favor of an heavy increase to our vessels of war, more than once finding himself upon the record in company with the Federalists under the lead of Josiah Quincy, rather than with his own party.

The war spirit continued to increase in and out of Congress, despite the opinions of the older and more cautious politicians who were averse to it, and who had, in their opposition, the undivided support of the Executive and the Cabinet. Madison, indeed, viewed a declaration of war with no favor, and only gave at last to the deputation of his political supporters who, with Clay at their head, waited upon him in a body, and demanded it as the necessary condition of his re-nomination to the Presidency, a timid and reluctant assent.

When the House re-assembled on the 2nd of November, 1812, Mr. Lowndes, who had already been elected to the ensuing Congress, was appointed to the Committee of Military Affairs, on which he served throughout the session as a zealous supporter of the war. He received in consequence, on the assembling of the Thirteenth Congress, 13th of December, 1813, the appointment of Chairman of Committee on Naval Affairs, and on the 4th of January following, having reported a resolution of honors to the Navy, made in support of it a speech, brief, yet so eloquent and stirring that it was received and read with enthusiasm in every part of the country. Nor can this kindling address, so happily conceived and so forcibly delivered, be read to-day without emotion. It deserves, too, an especial attention from the extensive popularity it gave to its author. Mr. Lowndes spoke as follows:

"I should be inexcusable if I were long to detain the committee from the vote—I hope the unanimous vote—which they are prepared to give upon the resolutions. The victories to which they refer are, indeed, of unequal magnitude and importance; but the least important of them, if it had been obtained by the subjects of any government on the continent of Europe, would have been heard with admiration and rewarded with munificence. I refer to the action between the Enterprise and the Boxer, from which the public eye appears to be withdrawn by the greater magnitude and the confessedly superior splendor of a more recent victory. * * * Although Lieut. Burroughs was mortally wounded early in the action, yet the skill and gallantry with which he commenced it, leave no doubt that if he had been longer spared to the wishes and wants of his country, the same brilliant result would have been obtained under his command; while the ability with which Lieut. McCall continued and completed the contest, assures to him as distinguished a fame as if he had carried the vessel into action. The loss of a commander, indeed, may fairly be considered as rendering a victory more honorable to a successor, because it must render it more difficult: it may be expected to confuse, though it may not depress.

"Of the victory of Lake Erie it is impossible for me to speak in terms which will convey any adequate conception of its importance, of the unrivalled excellence of the officers, and of the gratitude of the country.

"The documents referred to the committee sufficiently prove that superiority of force on the part of the enemy which would have insured their victory, if it were not the appropriate character of military genius to refute the calculations which rely on the superiority of force. Nor was the victory obtained over an unskilful and pusillanimous enemy. The English officers were brave and experienced, and the slaughter on board their vessels before they were surrendered, sufficiently attests the bravery of their seamen. They were skilful officers subdued by the ascendency of still superior skill.

* * * * * * * * * * * *

"There was one characteristic of this action which seems to me so strongly to distinguish it, that I cannot forbear to ask the attention of the committee to it for a few moments. I know no instance in naval or military history, in which the success of the contest appeared so obviously to result from the personal act of the commander as in this. When the crew of Capt. Perry's vessel lay bleeding around him; when his ship was a defenceless hospital, if he had wanted—not courage, which in an American officer forms no distinction—but if he had wanted that fertility of resource which extracts from disaster the means of success and glory, I do not say, if he had surrendered his ship, but if he had obstinately defended her, if he had gone down wrapped in his flag; if he had pursued any other conduct than that which he did pursue, his associates might have emulated his desperate courage, but they must have shared his fate. The battle was lost.

"Now examine any other victory, however brilliant. If, in the battle of the Nile, Lord Nelson had fallen even by the first fire, does any man believe that it would have affected the result of the contest? In the battle of Trafalgar he did fall, and Victory never for a moment fluttered from what was then her chosen eyrie—the British mast. And, not only in this view was the victory of Capt. Perry unrivalled, but in the importance even of its immediate consequences. I know none in the modern history of naval warfare that can be compared with it. An important territory immediately rescued from the grasp of English power—uppermost Canada conquered, or prepared for conquest; an ocean secured from the intrusion of every foreign flag; a frontier of a thousand miles relieved from the hostility of the most dreadful foe that civilized man has ever known! Nay, further, Capt. Perry and his gallant associates have not only given us victory in one quarter, but shown us how to obtain it in another yet more important

How deep is now the impression on every mind that we want but ships to give our fleet on the Atlantic the success which has hitherto attended our single vessels! We want but ships. We want then but *time*. Never had a nation, when first obliged to engage in the defence of naval rights by naval means—never had such a nation the advantages or the success of ours. The naval glory of other States has risen by continued effort—by slow gradation; that of the United States, almost without a dawn, has burst upon the world in all the sudden splendor of a tropical day. To such men we can do no honor. All records of the present time must be lost,—history must be a fable or a blank,—or their fame is secure. To the naval character of the country our votes can do no honor, but we may secure ourselves from the imputation of insensibility to its merit—we can at least express our admiration and our gratitude."

The first measure of importance brought up at this session had been the new and stringent Embargo Act. It became a law on the 17th of December, and provided for a strict embargo until the 1st of January, 1815, unless hostilities ceased meanwhile. The news of the battle of Leipsic and Napoleon's retreat across the Rhine, which was made known just before new-year's day, 1814, caused an immediate agitation in favor of its repeal by all who were in favor of peace, and who dreaded the advent of English armies in Canada, when released from service in Europe by the fall of Napoleon then thought to be imminent. Lord Castlereagh had at the same time written to Monroe, the Secretary of State, to express the willingness of the British government to treat for peace. Nor was it long before the Embargo Act was found to injure the country, whose commerce it paralyzed, and not the enemy, who had accumulated provisions for a whole year in advance. On the 14th of April, such was the pressure of the peace party, acting in concert with leading members who supported Mr. Lowndes in his opposition to any restrictions upon commerce, that the Act was repealed hardly four months after its passage.

The bills which were passed under Mr. Lowndes's influence at this session were laws—in aid of the naval establishment and the general system of national defence; to authorize an increase of the marine corps, and the construction of floating batteries; to allow rank to be bestowed on naval officers for distinguished conduct; to provide for the appointment of flotilla officers, for bounties for prisoners captured on the high seas and brought into port, and for pensions for the widows and children of those who were slain in action.

Although the treaty between England and the United States had been signed on the 24th of December, 1814, the despatches of our Commissioners did not reach America, as is well known, till the 11th of the following February, more than a month after the battle of New-Orleans. As fast as the news of peace was made known, the sound of rejoicings everywhere filled the air, and the roads leading into the large cities were alive with people hurrying to behold illuminations or to listen to the congratulations of party leaders.

The war had never been popular, for the sufferings and hardships it entailed had caused the grievances which led to it to be so far overlooked, that there were very few to grumble at their relinquishment by President Madison, in the final instructions to the American Commissioners. The country, however, soon saw and clearly understood that the reëstablishment of peace in Europe had removed that intense strain upon the resources of England which had caused its government to wink at the impressment of seamen from vessels belonging to the United States and the consequent dishonor to their flag. The American army had got no great amount of glory by the war, but had rather given promise of future distinction by its gallantry at Chippewa and its steadiness at Lundy's Lane. The navy had carried off the honors of the struggle, and was the popular arm of the service. Congressmen and politicians who had labored for it and supported it acquired an undoubted hold upon the favor of the people. They were well nigh the only class of public men who did.

Nor was England less willing to negotiate; for there had been from the outset a large party in the mother country, who, like the Federalists of the North, welcomed the treaty as "the conclusion of a destructive war which wisdom and temper might have entirely prevented." *

The unwise project of invasion had been tried upon the northern and southern border of the Union, and had failed through the victory of McDonough on Lake Champlain and Jackson at New-Orleans. While the defence of Canada and her supremacy upon the ocean were possible to England from the abundance and character of her resources, yet so distant was the scene of war, that she could only maintain hostilities at an enormous expenditure. Both countries desired peace so equally, that when peace was made, the contemporary historian wrote of the provisions of the treaty that "not the least notice was taken of any of the points at issue on the commencement of the war and which were the occasion of it; so that the continuance of peace must depend either upon the absence of those circumstances which produced the disputes, or upon a spirit of reciprocal moderation and conciliation, the desirable fruit of dear-bought experience." †

In place of the circumstances which led to the dispute, a wise spirit of conciliation has arisen among the educated statesmen of either country, which is gradually spreading among the people of both nations, leading to a study of their independent as well as their long common histories, and removing many of the misconceptions which had naturally sprung into existence, like baneful weeds in neglected ground, between two branches of the same race so long widely separated, and whose only intercourse had been on little other than cold or hostile terms.

While there were some among the public men who brought about the war, who suffered in popular opinion, it was the good fortune of Mr. Lowndes, from his diligence as chairman of the Naval Committee of the House, and his identification thereby, as it were, with the navy itself, to increase his reputation and strengthen the favor in which his name was held.

On the 4th of December, 1815, he was placed at the head of the Committee of Ways and Means. He served as its chairman for three years, and until he staid away from Washington, in November, 1818, in order to avoid re-appointment, not taking his seat until the second week of the session.‡

He voted for the reëstablishment of the United States Bank, when the measure was carried by the Republican adoption of the Federal argument that it was a necessary financial instrument of the government. Few questions have produced such violent controversy. The first bank had only received the approval of Washington, when the federal party was prepared to

---

\* Annual Register, vol. 57, p. 123.
† Ibid, p. 124.
‡ Memoirs J. Q. Adams, iv. p. 174.

pass it over his veto.* The Republican party which had abolished it as unconstitutional, were subsequently led by the embarrassments of the government during the war, the disorder of the currency, and the difficulty of taxation, to reverse their opinions and to regard its restoration as indispensable. At a later period, Mr. Lowndes, who had constantly supported the bank, defended its refusal to redeem the notes of one branch at any other,—wherever the holder might choose to present them,—and reviewed the whole subject of banking and exchange, after a long study of the subject, in a speech which was widely reprinted by the public journals. During the whole period of his service upon the Ways and Means, he was most diligent in committee, constant in attendance in the House, and a participant in every important debate.

On the 16th of October, 1816, he was invited by Madison to become a member of his cabinet as Secretary of War, but declined the honor. In the following year he was again offered by President Monroe the War portfolio, but he preferred his position as the leader of the House, and it was given, on his second declination of it, to Calhoun. The President's letter to Mr. Lowndes upon this subject has been preserved. It is interesting, since it serves to clearly indicate the considerations which formerly governed the selection of the cabinet. It reads :

*Confidential.* WASHINGTON, MAY 31, 1817.

DEAR SIR:

Having manifested my desire to draw into the administration, citizens of distinguished merit from each great section of the Union, and Governour Shelby who was appointed Secretary of War from the State of Kentucky having declined the appointment, I consider myself at liberty to look to other parts for aid, from those best qualified to afford it. On you my attention has in consequence been fixed, and I beg you to be assured that your acceptance of that office will be highly gratifying to me from personal as well as public considerations. As I am about to leave the city and shall be absent some time, I will thank you to be so good as to transmit your answer to me under cover of Mr. Rush, who will forward it to me.

I am, dear Sir, with great respect and esteem,
Your Obd't Sv't,
(signed) JAMES MONROE.

Mr. Lowndes also refused the mission to France, and again, a year later, the choice of the special missions to Constantinople and St. Petersburgh, which President Monroe, after consultation with John Quincy Adams, then Secretary of State, had offered to him.†

In 1818, he spoke almost every week of the session upon a great variety of subjects, and never failed to command the undivided attention of the House. On the 30th of January, 1819, he reviewed the whole subject of the Seminole War, and the course pursued by General Jackson in Florida, in a long but close reasoned speech, taking the ground that if Congress were to suppress its disapprobation of the occupation of St. Marks and Pensacola, it would not serve to raise in any way the the military character of General Jackson, but that it would impair its own character, its reputation and its dignity. He was chairman of the Committee on Coins and on Weights and

* Letter of James Madison to William Lowndes.
† Memoirs of J. Q. Adams, vol. v. p. 77.

Measures, and made upon these subjects numerous and elaborate notes, which show his thorough method of work in the preparation of reports to the House. He had however, for a long time, over-tasked himself, and was obliged to leave Washington in the spring of 1819, suffering greatly from exhaustion. By the advice of his physicians he sought restoration to health in the entire relaxation of a sea voyage, and, on landing at Liverpool, received the thoughtful, cordial, and generous welcome of an English gentleman, from the historian of the Medici, Mr. Roscoe. Intent upon self-improvement and knowledge, he remained at Liverpool until he had studied and recorded in his note-book everything which struck his curious and active mind. He found in the docks, the system of labor, the workshops, the commercial regulations, both of statute and local enactment, subjects worthy of careful examination and study, to be afterwards made available in the committee rooms of the Capitol.

He met, on one occasion, at Liverpool, a gentleman with whom he had a long conversation, and, under the English custom of intercourse without introduction, they separated without receiving it. Mr. Lowndes had so impressed himself upon the other, that the latter went immediately to Mr. Roscoe and inquired who the stranger was, describing him as the tallest man he had ever seen, the most unassuming he had ever met, and, certainly, the man of the greatest intellect he had ever heard speak. "It is the great American Lowndes you have been talking with; come and dine with me to-morrow, and I will introduce you to him." *

The journey to London gave him an opportunity to observe the agriculture of the midland counties. He visited Newmarket, went through the stables, and wrote down in his note-book everything he could learn about the care and improvement of horse-flesh, which he thought could be usefully adopted on his own side of the Atlantic. At London, he took every opportunity to visit the House of Commons, making the acquaintance of the parliamentary leaders, and watching their conduct of public business. On his departure from London he went directly to Paris, and there dined with Humboldt at Mr. Gallatin's table. He constantly attended the Chamber of Deputies, listened to their debates, and noted in his diary the characteristics of the Chamber, comparing it with the House of Commons. He thought its parliamentary rules well planned, and the French method of arresting debate by a direct vote to close the discussion seemed to him an improvement upon our own rule of the previous question. He travelled through France and Northern Italy, and returned to London after a tour through Holland and Belgium. Remaining but a short time in England on his way home, he took his seat on the 8th of December, two days after the assembly of the Sixteenth Congress. He received on the same day the appointment of chairman of the Committee on Foreign Affairs. On the 22d of February, 1820, he introduced a resolution, which was unanimously adopted, to authorize the report of a bill to confer upon the family of Commodore Perry the same pension that they would have been entitled to receive had Perry fallen in the battle of Lake Erie, instead of surviving for a few short years to die of yellow fever at Port Spain. Mr. Lowndes's speech on this occasion was written out by him on the evening after its delivery, at the request of his friend the Hon. Nathaniel Silsbee, of Massachusetts. It is noticeable as the only speech of the long series, comprehending every question of the

---

* "Reminiscences and Sketches," by E. S. Thomas, i. p. 103. The author gives this anecdote on the authority of Mr. Roscoe himself.

time, which he delivered during his congressional career, that ever received any revision at his hands.* As soon as the question upon the resolution had been put after he resumed his seat, John Randolph of Roanoke arose, to offer another resolution, the basis of the subsequent act, which provided not only for the support of Perry's family, but also for the education of his children. His remarks, very characteristic of the man and strongly put, were prefaced by these opening words of compliment,—a thing rare at any time from him,—to Mr. Lowndes. "Mr. Speaker, I believe it will prove a very difficult undertaking for any member of this House to keep pace with the honorable gentleman from South Carolina in the race of honor and public utility. It is certainly not possible for me to do so, for I have already been anticipated in a proposition which I desired to make to-day, because it is one eminently fit to introduce on this anniversary so inspiring to patriotic emotions."

Mr. Lowndes spoke at this session on the Missouri Compromise, against Mr. Clay's resolutions on the Spanish treaty, and in opposition to the revision of the Tariff. When Mr. Clay resigned the speakership, at the opening of the second session in November, 1820, Mr. Lowndes became the candidate of his party against Mr. John W. Taylor, of New-York. At the close of the ballot on the second day of the session he lacked but one vote of an election. Fourteen votes had been diverted by the candidacy of Gen. Smith, of Maryland. "a man ruined in fortune and reputation, yet who commanded votes enough," as John Quincy Adams recorded in his diary on the evening of that day, "to defeat the election of Lowndes, a man of irreproachable character, amiable disposition and popular manners."

Mr. Taylor was chosen Speaker on the next ballot, and on the 23d of November, Mr. Lowndes, who had been appointed chairman of the select committee on the proposed constitution of Missouri, reported a bill for her admission to the Union. Its consideration was set down for the 6th of December, and the whole country awaited the debate with a deeper interest than it had given to any subject since the adoption of the constitution. It was the first great encounter on the question of slavery, and the South, more distinguished then in the superior weight and character of her delegations in the House, than at any other period of her long supremacy—if we accept the recorded opinion of him, then, too, illustrious in every branch of the public service, yet destined to attain his own most enviable honors years afterwards in that House as the worthiest champion of the North—the South, grasping the situation with the keenest comprehension of its magnitude, entrusted the presentation and management of her cause to Mr. Lowndes, the wisest since he was the most moderate of all her public men.

Of his speech, in opening the debate, there is left to us in the annals of Congress only an insufficient abstract. His opening sentences were lost to the official reporters of the House, as Mr. Benton tells us in his note upon the speech, by the movement of representatives from every part of the chamber, as they hurriedly changed their seats to get near the speaker, and catch every word that fell from his lips, "Mr. Lowndes being one of those so rare in every assembly around whom members clustered when he rose to speak, that not a word should be lost where every word was luminous with intelligence and captivating with candor. This clustering around him, always the case with Mr. Lowndes when he rose to speak, was

* Abridgment of Debates, vol. vii. p. 346.

more than usually eager on this occasion from the circumstances under which he spoke;—the Union verging to dissolution, and his own condition verging to the grave." *

The debate lasted through the winter, and it was not till the 28th of February, 1821, that the State of Missouri was conditionally admitted to the Union, and the second Missouri question compromised like the first.†

During the greater portion of the winter Mr. Lowndes was confined to his residence by severe illness, the premonition of the end to come two years later. The management of the Missouri question, owing to his inability to attend the House, was entrusted by him to Mr. Clay, who frequently conferred with him in his chamber in regard to it. The compromise became thus the work, as it was the fortunate opportunity of Henry Clay. He availed himself of the weakness of the Northern position to undermine it, and dissension was, for a few years, allayed. Mr. Lowndes spoke but rarely after his recovery, once or twice when able to attend the House on some point in the Missouri debate, and once in favor of an inquiry into the Bankrupt Laws. He was under medical observation during the summer of 1821, and rallied somewhat before he returned to Washington, which was not until the 21st of December, nearly three weeks after the opening of the Seventeenth Congress, having once more kept away at the organization of the House to avoid the chairmanship of a committee. In the last week of December, at a caucus of the Legislature of South Carolina, he received its nomination for the Presidency. This movement of his native state was an entire surprise to him. His answer, which passed into a proverb, and was destined to be the speech by which he will be longest remembered, is best given in a letter to his wife, written at Washington, 6th January, 1822. "You have heard of the caucus nomination at Columbia. I hope you have not set your mind too strongly on being President's lady. While you wish only a larger fence for the poultry yard, and a pond for the ducks, I may be able to gratify you, but this business of making a President either of oneself or of another I have no cunning at. We live in a terrible confusion. I thought when I came here the question was a fact confined to two persons, Mr. Crawford and Mr. Adams. Now, we have all the secretaries and at least two who are not to be named. As to the answer which I have made to the notification, here it is: 'I have taken no step and never shall to draw the public attention upon me as a competitor for the Presidency. It is not in my opinion an office to be either solicited or declined.'"

Mr. Lowndes served at this session on the Committee on the Mint and the Coinage, and spoke for the last time in Congress on the 22d of March, 1822, on a resolution authorizing an exchange of government bonds.

He continued to decline in vigor, under the debilitating influence of disease and the method of treatment adopted in his case. The strength of the overworked statesman at length gave way entirely. He resigned in the autumn his seat in Congress, and sailed in October in the ship Moss, from Philadelphia. Accompanied by his wife and daughter, he hoped to find, in a longer absence from home, and in the choice of climate which Europe afforded, restoration of health. It was not thus to be. He grew rapidly worse, and died on the 27th of October, when he had been but nine days at sea. The news of his death, which occasioned universal concern and sorrow,

---

\* Abridgment of Debates, vol. vii. p. 12.
† Memoirs of J. Q. Adams, vol. v. p. 307.

did not reach the United States till the 11th of January, 1823. Ten days later, on the 21st of the month, the House of Representatives, of which, at his death, he was not a member, and in which James Hamilton, Jr. already sat as his successor, passed the same resolutions of respect to his memory, and of mourning for his loss, which they would have done had he fallen like the second Adams upon its floor. The eulogies upon him of Hamilton, and Archer, and Taylor are among the most beautiful of such efforts. Hamilton declared that his wisdom was equalled only by his moderation, that he had less self-love and more self-denial than any other man he had known. Archer described his character as one in which the qualities that win esteem were blended in the happiest way with those that command it. Taylor, of New-York, affirmed that the highest and best hopes of the country had looked to William Lowndes for their fulfilment, that the Chief Magistracy would have been illustrated by his virtues and talents. " During nine years," said Mr. Taylor, " I have served with him on many important committees, and he never failed to shed new light on all the subjects to which he applied his vigorous and discriminating mind. To manners the most unassuming, to patriotism the most disinterested, to morals the most pure, to attainments of the highest order in literature and science, he added the virtues of decision and prudence so happily combined, so harmoniously united, that we knew not which most to admire, the firmness with which he pursued his purpose, or the gentleness by which he disarmed opposition. You, Mr. Speaker," he concluded, " will remember his zeal in sustaining the cause of our country in the darkest days of our late war. You cannot have forgotten—who that heard him can ever forget the impression of his eloquence in announcing the resolutions of thanks to the gallant Perry for the victory on Lake Erie? Alas! Alas! the statesman has joined the hero,—never—never again shall his voice be heard in this Hall."

Said the National Intelligencer of the following day: " The tribute, which was yesterday paid to the memory of the lamented William Lowndes, is as honorable to the feeling of the House as it is to the memory of the deceased. The brief addresses, delivered on the occasion, were such as worthily became the speakers, and never perhaps was eulogy more justly or more disinterestedly bestowed."

For the period of one month, in accordance with their resolution, the House wore, as a badge of mourning, crape upon the left arm. This action, which had been without precedent in the annals of the House, has served as its example since that time, on the few occasions that the House has been called upon to pay especial honor to the memory of a great citizen who was not at the time of his death a member of their own body.

Not less deep and earnest than the tributes of the House were the later words of Mr. R. H. Wilde, subsequently Professor of the University of Louisiana, in his " Sketches of Members of the Fourteenth Congress."

" Preëminent, yet not more proudly than humbly preëminent among them was a gentleman from South Carolina, now no more: the purest, the calmest, the most philosophical of our country's modern statesmen, one no less remarkable for gentleness of manners and kindness of heart than for that passionless unclouded intellect which rendered him deserving, if ever man deserved it, of merely standing by and letting reason argue for him. The true patriot, incapable of all self-ambition, who shunned office and distinction, yet served his country faithfully because he loved her,—he, I mean, who consecrated by his example the noble precept so entirely his own, that the first station in the Republic was neither to be sought after nor declined, a sentiment so just and so happily expressed that it continues to be repeated because it cannot be improved."

Nor is the deliberate opinion of the graver historian less warm. Benton, who said of Mr. Lowndes, that his opinion had a weight never exceeded by that of any other American statesman, who wrote at a period when almost all who had ever served with him in Congress had passed away, and whose personal acquaintance with him had been but slight, since he commenced his own long career at the time that declining health had led to Mr. Lowndes's resignation, devotes to his character and influence one of the opening chapters of his work.

"All that I saw of him confirmed the impression of the exalted character which the public voice had ascribed to him. Virtue, modesty, benevolence, patriotism, were the qualities of his heart; a sound judgment, a mild, persuasive elocution were the attributes of his mind; his manners gentle, natural, cordial, and inexpressibly engaging. He was one of the galaxy, as it was well called, of the brilliant young men whom South Carolina sent to the House of Representatives at the beginning of the war of 1812.—Calhoun, Cheves, Lowndes,—and was soon the brightest star in that constellation. * * * He was the moderator as well as the leader of the House, and was followed by its sentiment in all cases in which inexorable party feeling or some powerful interest did not rule the action of the members, and even then he was courteously and deferentially treated. It was so the only time I ever heard him speak,—session of 1820-21, and on the inflammable subject of the admission of the State of Missouri. His death was a public and national calamity."*

When Mr. Clay was asked, towards the close of his long life, by Colonel John Lee, of Maryland, who, of all the public men he had known, was in his opinion the greatest, he replied that it was difficult to decide among the many whom he had been associated with, but, said he, "I think the wisest man I ever knew was William Lowndes."

Ex-President Van Buren, towards the end of that work which occupied his later years, and which he did not live to see published,† in speaking of the protective system, which had its origin in the prolific mind of Hamilton, says: "The enforcement of Hamilton's recommendations was reserved for the close of the war of 1812, a period of which I have already spoken as one which brought on the political stage a new class of Presidential aspirants, members of a succeeding generation and unknown to Revolutionary fame. Among the most prominent of these stood Crawford, Clay, Calhoun, Adams, Webster and Lowndes,—the latter, perhaps, the most likely to have succeeded, if his useful life had not been brought to a premature close."

Such are some of the opinions given of this most highly gifted man. He was a descendant, let it be here said, of the same family as was his distinguished namesake, William Lowndes, Secretary of the Treasury to Queen Anne. This statesman, the author of the British funding system, rose to influence of the first rank by service upon the Committee of Ways and Means in the House of Commons. By a curious and striking coincidence, a century later, the subject of our sketch, as chairman of a similar committee in the House of Representatives, earned the same designation in the annals of the

---

\* Benton. "Thirty years View," vol. i. pp. 9, 10, 15.
† "Political Parties in the United States," pp. 115-16.

United States that the other had won as the " Ways and Means Lowndes " of the Parliamentary History of England, and thus, long ago, there sprang from the old manor house of Legh Hall in Cheshire, offshoots of that family, which had been even then long associated with its walls, that were destined to carry in after time their common name high into the councils of each of the great families of the English race.

To the student of the constitutional history of the United States, the life and character of William Lowndes, although it may be utterly forgotten among the people, will always have a peculiar interest from the numerous possibilities which associate themselves with it and which were extinguished at his death. He was called "an old statesman " by the press, and yet he was but forty when he died. He had never served the country but as a member of the lower House of Congress, rejecting in turn the summons of Madison and Monroe to their cabinets, and the offers of three foreign missions, yet it is safe to say that the Union has never, in this the first century of its independence, lost another statesman of his age who made so deep an impression upon its affection and judgment, and who left so enviable a fame. His last public act, as it might be called, such is the temper of the Republic towards all who have incurred her suspicion of unduly striving for the Presidency, and in such sharp contrast was his attitude to that assumed by his three great contemporaries, Webster, Clay, and Calhoun,—the dignified position he took in reference to his nomination,—won for him a feeling of personal admiration, even from his opponents, which was expressed long afterwards in conversation and private correspondence whenever his character and attainments were the subject of affectionate and interesting reminiscence.

The personal appearance of Mr. Lowndes was remarkable; for his stature exceeded six feet and six inches, and he was as slender as he was tall. Though loose limbed he managed his length easily. His features were large, while the face was thin, long and pale. He was habitually grave and thoughtful, and never relaxed into idle conversation or even social raillery, yet—*comitate condita gravitas*—he was neither solemn nor severe, and his smile, though rare, was said to be inexpressibly engaging. His habitual seriousness was relieved by the presence of his children, and he was always cheerful when they were with him or came to be tossed in his long arms. Present or absent, says Mr. Grayson, they were objects of tender solicitude. He found time to correspond with them even during the labors attendant upon a session of Congress, and watched their progress as evidenced by their letters. He urged them to be diligent by appeals to their filial affection rather than to their desire of emulation. His manners and address were full of dignity, and he was as invariably courteous in private life as he was in his public career. How distinctively he may be said to have earned his public reputation for these qualities we have already seen, yet it is well to notice the valuable opinion of the distinguished historian of the Abolition Party, the late Vice-President of the United States, who speaks of Mr. Lowndes " as one of the ablest and certainly one of the most courteous and moderate Southern statesmen."[*]

While sought in society by its most conspicuous members, and honored by the friendship of his elders in years and station, he was always a peculiar favorite of men and women younger than himself. He had from natural modesty rather than from cultivation that faculty of deferent attention to

---

[*] " Rise and Fall of the Slave Power," by Henry Wilson, i. p. 158.

others which wins in social intercourse at once confidence and regard. The late Mr. John Ravenel sometimes told the following anecdote in illustration of the attachment Mr. Lowndes inspired among young people:—Mr. Ravenel was the pupil of a Major Wilson, a surveyor, and had been sent by him into the neighborhood of El Dorado, the estate of General Thomas Pinckney. He was at once asked by the General to his house. A youth and a stranger, he felt and perhaps betrayed something of natural embarrassment incidental to his position in the company at General Pinckney's table, when a tall gentleman, who was entirely unknown to him, engaged his attention, and delighted him by the charm of his manner, and by his agreeable conversation. He soon learned that the tall gentleman was his host's son-in-law, and the leader of the congressional delegation of his State.* As he was considerate and attentive to others, he was modest in his own share of conversation; and, while insensibly guiding it, never took the exclusive control which would so often have been willingly accorded him. Conversation in his presence never became monologue. He was in no sense disputatious, and talked for the sake of truth and not for victory. Whether in the drawing-room, in committee, or in the House, he never became heated nor vehement, but turned an angry disputant by calm remark and gentle manner.

When once asked by a gentleman long noted for colloquial skill, what but failure would be the fate of the American Republic; what would be the condition of things when there came to be more than thirty states; how could faction be controlled, where could safeguards be found in a democracy to protect the liberties of the people, Mr. Lowndes, to whom it would have been easy as one hopeful of the Union to reply in "glittering generalities," quietly observed, "That the people of that future time would be so much better informed than he could be of the evils approaching and their remedies, that he was entirely content to leave the whole subject for them to examine and arrange."

Without despising popular opinion, he placed no great value either on its praise or its censure, and was entirely undisturbed by the occasional attacks of party journals. It was Mr. Rutledge who related of him the story that once, while on a journey with Mr. Lowndes through Pennsylvania, they stopped a short time at a village, and that a stranger to them in the hotel, who seemed to be a prominent character in the town, after listening to their conversation, came up to Mr. Lowndes and asked him as a favor to run his eye over a communication he had prepared for the country newspaper and give him the benefit of his corrections. Mr. Lowndes, on reading the article, found it to be an attack upon the administration and its leading supporters, and especially virulent upon himself. He corrected and returned the paper without intimating who he was, and then asked the writer what reason he had for abusing Mr. Lowndes. "None at all," was the reply, "but I don't believe any man ever possessed so many good qualities as are imputed to him by all parties." † From this slight incident we may infer his estimate of popular censure and applause.

His oratory was easy, unaffected, and refined in manner. It made a deep impression upon his audience by its contrast with the more florid style of the period in which he lived. In the State House at Columbia he was always heard with profound attention. His manner was calm and persuasive, his action subdued, his style clear and flowing, his voice good but not strong. He made no questionable rhetorical flights, but seemed to the

* Mr. F. J. Grayson. † Ibid.

listener to be animated solely with the desire to ascertain and enforce the truth. He was remarkable in debate for a candor that never failed to see and acknowledge the strength of an opponent's argument. He would freely admit what an inferior mind would have striven only to elude, and would always concede all that his adversary's argument could demand. His practice in debate was to state at the outset, fully and clearly, the strong points of the speech to which he had risen to reply. Mr. Alfred Huger related that, on some occasions, Mr. Lowndes would put his adversary's argument with such force that his own friends would become alarmed lest he might fail to pull down what he had so firmly erected. The fear was needless, even on the occasion when John Randolph of Roanoke, who was opposed to him, had declared aloud on the floor of the House, as Mr. Lowndes went on, that the speaker had entrapped himself and would never answer his own argument. Mr. Randolph, however, at the end of the speech, admitted that he had been mistaken.

Fortunate as Mr. Lowndes was in his public career, he was not the less happy in his private relations. No censure ever assailed his domestic life, for he was known of all men to be pure.

Mr. Lowndes married, ———, 1802, Elizabeth-Brenton, daughter of General Thomas Pinckney.* By this lady, who died in July, 1857, Mr. Lowndes had:

    i. RAWLINS,[8] b. 1804; m. ———, 1827, Emma-Raymond Hornby, and died s. p. ———, 1834.
18. ii. THOMAS-PINCKNEY,[8] b. Oct. —, 1808.
    iii. REBECCA-MOTTE,[8] b. ———, 1810; m. June 16, 1829, to Edward-L. Rutledge, of the Navy, and has issue:
        i. HARRIOTT-HORRY,[9] m. ———, 1851, St. Julien-Ravenel, and has issue:
            i. *Harriott-Rutledge*,[10] b. 1852.
            ii. *Anna-Eliza*,[10] b. 1853.
            iii. *John*,[10] b. 1856.
            iv. *Elizabeth-Rutledge*,[10] b. 1857.
            v. *Edward-Rutledge*,[10] b. 1859.
            vi. *St.-Julien*,[10] b. 1861.
            vii. *Frances-Gualdo*,[10] b. 1865.
            viii. *Francis-Gualdo*,[10] b. 1869.
            ix. *Helen-Lowndes*,[10] b. 1872.
    ii. ELIZABETH-PINCKNEY,[9] b. 1812; died in infancy.

12. RAWLINS[8] LOWNDES, now the senior representative of the family which has been the subject of this sketch, was educated at the United States Military Academy at West Point, which he entered August 31, 1816. He was graduated 1st July, 1820, and promoted in the Army to the rank of 2d Lieutenant, Corps of Cavalry. He was stationed at Fort Moultrie in the winter of 1820, and was on topographical duty in 1821, in the valley of the Missouri, at that time a pathless waste of prairie. He was appointed Aide-

---

* Thomas Pinckney was born in Charleston, 23d October, 1750. The child of wealthy parents, he received a thorough classical education in England. He was conspicuous at the outbreak of the Revolution, and on the assumption by Gates of the command of the Southern Army was appointed his aide. When the army was defeated at the battle near Camden, Major Pinckney, whose leg had been shattered by a musket ball, was taken prisoner. He succeeded General Moultrie as Governor of South Carolina in 1787. In 1792 he received the appointment of Minister Plenipotentiary to Great Britain, and in 1794 was sent with the same rank to Spain to treat in reference to the navigation of the Mississippi. In 1800 he was chosen Member of Congress. At the commencement of the second war with England, Dearborn, having received the appointment of Commander-in-Chief, and been assigned to the Northern Army, Pinckney was commissioned as Major General and placed in command of the Southern Department. At the end of the war he retired to his plantation, El Dorado, where he died on the 2d of November, 1828.

de-Camp, with the rank of Major, to Brevet-Major General Gaines, July 1, 1821, and remained on the staff of this officer till Dec. 31, 1830, when he resigned from the army, and returned to Carolina.

Here at his plantation, The Strip, on the North Santee River, for a period of thirty years, Major Lowndes resided during a portion of each year, returning to his town residence in New-York in the spring. In 1860, having purchased a small estate on the east bank of the Hudson, near to and between the old family seats of the Livingston family, into which he had married, he gave up his town residence, and, a few months later, in April, 1861, was forced to abandon his Carolina estate to swift destruction from neglect and the plunder of marauders, when the sea coast of the state became the scene of active war.

Since the year 1861, Major Lowndes has resided upon the Hudson River. He married, October 24, 1826, Gertrude-Laura, daughter of Maturin Livingston and Margaret Lewis his wife, only daughter and heiress of Morgan Lewis,* a Major General in the Army in the last war with England, son of Francis Lewis, a Signer of the Declaration of Independence, and by her has issue:

  i. JULIA-LIVINGSTON,[9] m. May 19, 1853, William-Augustus James, of Lynwood, near Rhinebeck-on-Hudson, and had issue:
    i. WILLIAM-LOWNDES,[10] b. June 1, 1855.
  Mrs. James died January 26, 1875.

  ii. MARY-LIVINGSTON,[9] m. January 31, 1855, John-Pyne March, son of the late Charles March, of Greenland, New-Hampshire. By her husband, who died November 25, 1873, she had issue:
    i. CHARLES,[10] b. September 23, 1856.
    ii. CLEMENT,[10] b. November 21, 1862.

  iii. GERTRUDE-LEWIS,[9] b. September 22, 1833; d. October 26, 1834.

  iv. ANNE,[9] m. George-B. Chase, of Boston [Harv. Coll. 1856], son of the late Theodore Chase, of Portsmouth, New-Hampshire, and afterwards of Boston, and has issue:
    i. STEPHEN,[10] b. January 30, 1863.
    ii. GERTRUDE-LOWNDES.[10]

  v. HARRIETT-LOWNDES,[9] m. April 27, 1859, Eugene Langdon, son of the late Walter Langdon, of Portsmouth, New-Hampshire, and has issue:

---

* Upon the east wall in St. James's Church, Hyde-Park-on-Hudson, N. Y., there is a mural tablet with this inscription:

To the Memory of
Major General MORGAN LEWIS,
Younger son of
Francis Lewis,
A Signer of the Declaration of Independence:
Born in New York, Oct. 16, 1754,
Died April 7, 1844.
In 1775, he enlisted as a volunteer in the army investing Boston.
In 1777, he served under General Gates, as Chief of his Staff,
and received the surrender of Burgoyne.
He conducted the retreat from Ticonderoga,
led the advance at Stone Arabia,
and was in active service till the close of the war.
In 1783, he commenced the practice of the Law,
and became Attorney General, Chief Justice, and
Governor of his Native State.
Under his administration the foundation was laid for our public school fund.
In 1812, as Major General, he served through the second war.
He was, for many years, Senior Warden of this Church,
and at the period of his death, was President of the Cincinnati,
and Grand Master of the Masons.
Warned by advancing years, with a mind unimpaired,
He retired from public life to the quiet of his family,
Where living and beloved, he went down to the grave
In a good old age, and in the fulness of honors.

i. MARION.[10]   ii. ANNE-LOWNDES.[10]

Mr. Langdon died Februrary 22, 1866. Mrs. Langdon m. secondly, November 2, 1872, Philip Schuyler, of New-York.

13. THOMAS[8] LOWNDES was graduated at Harvard College, 1824; m. February 12, 1828, Allen, daughter of Henry and Margaret Deas, of Charleston, by whom he had issue:
  i. HENRY,[9] b. January 29, 1829.   ii. SARAH-ION.[9]
  iii. THOMAS,[9] b. September 26, 1842; d. 18—.

Mr. Lowndes died July 8, 1833.

14. WILLIAM-PRICE[8] LOWNDES, educated at New-Haven, and afterwards at Columbia College, South Carolina; m. October 30, 1833, Susan-Mary-Elizabeth, daughter of Maturin and Margaret (Lewis) Livingston, of Staatsburgh, New-York, who died in New-York, February 10, 1875. By her he had issue:
  i. MARGARET,[9] m. June 6, 1865, Edward-Henry Costar, of the City of New-York, and has issue.
  ii. FRANCIS-LEWIS,[9] b. August 8, 1837; now a Councillor-at-Law, of the City of New-York.
  iii. WILLIAM,[9] b. August 1, 1843; m. May 22, 1875, Katherine-Grant, daughter of Daniel Ranson, of New-York.

15. CHARLES-TIDYMAN[8] LOWNDES, m. December 31, 1829, Sabina-Elliott, daughter of Daniel-Elliott and Isabella Huger, by whom he had issue:
  i. DANIEL-HUGER,[9] b. February 27, 1832; d. August 1, 1832.
  ii. DANIEL-HUGER,[9] b. June, 1833; d. January 9, 1835.
  iii. MARY-HUGER,[9] m. Edward-Laight Cottenet, of New-York, and has issue.
  iv. RAWLINS,[9] b. July 23, 1838; m. ———, Sarah, daughter of General John-S. Preston, of Virginia, now a resident on the family estate, Oaklands Parish of St. Bartholomew's, South Carolina.
  v. SABINA-HUGER,[9] m. William-Harleston Huger, M.D., of Charleston.
  vi. EMMA-HUGER.[9]

16. RICHARD-HENRY[8] LOWNDES, entered the Navy in 1831, served on the Brazils in the Lexington, as Aide to Com. A.-J. Dallas, in the Constellation, and as Aide to Com. Hull, in the Ohio, when flag-ship of the Mediterranean Squadron. Mr. Lowndes resigned in 1842. He m. Nov. 10, 1845, Susan-Middleton Parker, daughter of John and Emily (Rutledge) Parker, of Charleston, and has issue:
  i. CAROLINE,[9] m. Nov. 10, 1870, Dominic-Lynch Pringle, son of the Hon. John-Julius and Jane [Lynch] Pringle, and by him has issue.
  ii. RICHARD-ION,[9] b. Dec. 13, 1847; m Nov. 15, 1870, Alice-Izard, dau. of Ralph-Izard and Charlotte-Georgina [Izard] Middleton, and has issue:
    i. WILLIAM,[10] b. Aug. 10, 1872.
  iii. EMILY-RUTLEDGE,[9] m. Nov. 7, 1874, Charles-Petigru Allston, son of the Hon. R.-F.-W. and Adele (Petigru) Allston, and by him has issue.
  iv. WILLIAM-AIKEN,[9] b. April 20, 1856; d. April 23, 1863.

17. EDWARD-RUTLEDGE[8] LOWNDES, m., 1833, Mary-Lucia Guerard, and by her had issue:
  i. JAMES,[9] b. Jan. 6, 1835; was graduated at South Carolina College, Dec. 1854, and afterward a student at Heidelburg. Councillor-at-Law; served on the staff of the Confederate Army; resumed the practice of the law as partner of the Hon A. G. Magrath, in Charleston, in 1866; now a member of the bar of the District of Columbia, and resides at Washington.
  ii. EDWARD,[9] b. 1836; m. Celestina Fuller, and had:
    i. EDWARD-RUTLEDGE.[10]   ii. RAWLINS.[10]   iii. ALICE.[10]
  iii. MARY-LUCIA.[9]   iv. EMILY.[9]   v. ELIZABETH.[9]   vi. SOPHIA-PERCY.[9]

vii. JULIA,[9] m. William Hamilton.   viii. MARY-RUTH.[9]
ix. CATHERINE-HAMILTON.[9]

Mr. Lowndes died 1853.

18. THOMAS-PINCKNEY[8] LOWNDES, m. ———, 1829, Margaret-M., daughter of William and Martha (Blake) Washington, of Charleston, and granddaughter of Colonel William Washington, of the Revolutionary Army. By whom he had:

    i. JANE-WASHINGTON,[9] m. May 18, 1854, Robert-William Hume, and has issue:
        i. MARY-MORSE,[10] b. 1858.
        ii. MARGARET-LOWNDES,[10] b. 1859.
        iii. WILLIAM-LOWNDES,[10] b. 1863.
        iv. JANE-WASHINGTON,[10] b. 1871.
    ii. WILLIAM,[9] b. 1832; d. at Heidelberg, Germany. 1856.
    iii. THOMAS-PINCKNEY,[9] b. Feb 22. 1839; m. Nov. 9, 1865, Anne-Branford Frost, daughter of the Hon. Edward Frost, of South Carolina, and Harriet-Horry his wife, by whom Mr. Lowndes has issue:
        i HARRIET-HORRY,[10] b. Oct. 1866.
        ii. MARGARET-WASHINGTON,[10] b. May, 1869.
        iii. WILLIAM,[10] b. Oct. 1871.
        iv. EDWARD-FROST,[10] b. March, 1874.

Mr. Lowndes died in 1838.

ARMS OF RAWLINS LOWNDES, President of South Carolina in 1778. Quarterly of six.

LOWNDES.—Argent fretty azure, on a canton gules a lion's erased, or.
WELD.—Azure, a fesse nebule, between three crescents, ermine.
WETTENHALL.—Vert—a cross engrailed, ermine.
LIVERSAGE.—Argent, a chevron between three plough-shares erect, sable.
WHELOCK.—Argent, a chevron between three catherine wheels, sable.
RAWLINS.*

NOTE.—CHARLES[5] LOWNDES (page 12), the ancestor of the Carolina family, died in Charleston, March 27, 1736. Among the persons named in his will, occur the well-known names Arthur Middleton, Ralph Izard, Colonel Blake, Nathaniel Broughton, and Hon. John Colleton, Esq., cousin of Sir John Colleton, Baronet, one of the original Lords Proprietors of the Province.

---

It has not been deemed within the limits and scope of this memoir to trace in detail the descent of other branches of the Cheshire family of Lowndes, nor to endeavor, by a long and uncertain search, to carry the strict pedigree of the Bostock line back to a period anterior to that given by the English representatives of the family to Mr. Burke or his son for incorporation either in the History of the Commoners or in any of their later productions. A brief sketch, however, of the several branches of this old county family, with such mention of them as the local histories afford, may have some interest for American readers, especially as it embodies

* It has not been possible to ascertain with certainty the seal of the St. Kitts family of this name. In tropical climates wax impressions are rarely used, and can never be preserved. A wafer impression from the seal of Mr. Henry Rawlins is too faint to authorize any description of the arms of his family.

some facts which throw light upon other early settlements in the colonies by representatives of the Lowndes name.

To recur to the records of Lowndes of Bostock House, which, in tracing the pedigree of the Carolina branch, was brought down to RICHARD[4] LOWNDES, gent., of Bostock House, who succeeded his father, JOHN[3] LOWNDES, on the death of the latter, May 18, 1667, and who was baptized on the 13th of October, 1645.

He married ———— and had issue :
 i. MARY,[5] bapt. Oct. 25, 1670; m. Feb. 3, 1690, John Kelso, Esq., of the City of Chester.
 ii. RICHARD,[5] his heir.
 iii. WILLIAM,[5] bapt. Sept. 30, 1678.
 iv. ALICE,[5] bapt. June 1, 1683.
 v. FRANCES,[5] bapt. Sept. 2, 1684.
 vi. THOMAS,[5] bapt. Sept. 25, 1686.

Mr. Lowndes died January 14, 1709, and was succeeded by his elder son, RICHARD[5] LOWNDES, Esq., of Bostock House and Hassall Hall, baptized Oct. 17, 1673, who m. Margaret, daughter of ———— Poole, gent., of a younger branch of the Pooles, of Poole, in the county of Chester, and had issue :
 i. MARGARET,[6] bapt. Sept. 21, 1697.
 ii. KATHERINE,[6] bapt. Oct. 7, 1699; died unmarried.
 iii. FRANCES,[6] bapt. March 26, 1701; d. Nov. 9, 1716, unmarried.
 iv. RICHARD,[6] of Bostock House and Hassall Hall, bapt. April 8, 1703.
 v. WILLIAM,[6] of whom hereafter.
 vi. JOHN,[6] bapt. May 23, 1707; m. Mary, daughter of John Houghton, gent of Baguley, and had issue.
 vii. ELLEN,[6] bapt. August 16, 1709; died May 21, 1735, unmarried.
 viii. CHARLES,[6] bapt. August 27, 1711.
 ix. CHRISTOPHER,[6] bapt. June 19, 1713. Settled in America.
 x. ANNE,[6] bapt. Oct. 6, 1715.
 xi. EDWARD,[6] bapt. Jan. 22, 1717.
 xii. THOMAS,[6] bapt. Oct. 22, 1720; died unmarried.
 xiii. FRANCIS,[6] bapt. March 28, 1721.

Mr. Lowndes made his will on the 21st of February, 1726, and settled his estate of Bostock House on his eldest son Richard for life, and his heirs general, in consequence of which it descended to the two daughters and co-heirs of Richard Lowndes, Jun. Esq. Through the marriage of his father, he had succeeded to the representation and property of the eldest branch of the ancient family of Weld, now represented in the male line by the Welds of Lulworth Castle, in the county of Dorset. This property, Weld House and the Hall of Hassall, with adjoining estates, he settled on his eldest son for life and then on his heirs male; in fault of which, on his younger sons in tail male, but reserving a power to trustees to lease, in order to raise portions for younger children. The trustees did so for 500 years, and transferred the term to Richard Lowndes, the son, who left the leasehold interest to the daughters before mentioned. The free hold and reversion, however, remained with William Lowndes, the second son, whose grandson and heir, the late William Lowndes, Esq., in 1819 purchased the term, and thus became possessed of the family estate.

Mr. Lowndes died August 30, 1744. His second son, WILLIAM[6] LOWNDES,* gent., of Sandbach, baptized August 11, 1705,

* History of the Commoners, iv. p. 334.

m. September 24, 1740, Anne, eldest daughter and co-heir of William Berington, of Sandbach, gent. (by Anne, daughter and heir of Thomas Fletcher of Creswellshaw), descended from the ancient family of Berington, alias Barrington, of Bradwall, in the county of Chester, and by her, who died April 9, 1788, aged eighty-two years, left at his decease, May 15, 1789, an only son and successor,

WILLIAM[7] LOWNDES, Esq., of Sandbach, baptized June 9, 1744, who m. December 2, 1789, at Astbury, in the county of Chester, Susanna Sydebothom, daughter and heir to John Kirkby, gent., of Congleton, (descended from the Sydebothoms, of Northenden, in Cheshire), and by her, who died December 14, 1804, aged fifty, had issue:

   i.  WILLIAM,[8] his heir.
  ii.  JOHN-SYDEBOTHOM,[8] born May 13, 1798, and died November 23, 1819, aged twenty-one.
 iii.  ANNE-BARRINGTON,[8] m. July 22, 1818, at Astbury, to William Reddall, of Liverpool, gent., and has a daughter Susanna Kirkby[9] Reddall.

Mr. Lowndes was one of the deputy lieutenants for the county of Chester. He died, Nov. 7, 1806, and was succeeded by his eldest son.

WILLIAM LOWNDES,[8] Esq., of Hassall Hall, born October 27, 1795. He married, Sept. 13, 1827, Mary Elizabeth, daughter of William Smith, Esq., of Lichfield, and, dying without issue, left his property, papers, and the representation of his family to his niece, Miss

SUSANNA KIRKBY[9] REDDALL, now of Parnelscraft, Congleton.

ARMS AND CREST. Same as those of Lowndes of South Carolina.

*Estates.*—The Manor and Hall Estate, of Hassall: Creswellshaw: lands in Sandbach: Betchton: Astbury: and Congleton, all in the county of Chester.

---

We have already seen that the Carolina family trace their descent from William Lowndes, a descendant of a younger son of the family of LOWNDES of *Overton,* who was born possibly as late as the middle of the sixteenth century, and who died in 1590. There was living at Overton* about this time, in possession of that estate, as appears by a pedigree preserved in the Harleian manuscripts, No. 1505, fol. 336 and 197,† a William Lowndes, who traced his descent from

JOHN[1] LOWNDES of the same place, born about 1500, who married a daughter of —— Sherman of Smallwood in the same county, and had, among others, a son and heir,

RICHARD[2] LOWNDES, of Overton, who married Isabel, daughter of —— Lawden, of Gosty Hill, and left a son, the

---

\* Overton Hall, in the township of Smallwood, and parish of Astbury, about three miles south-east from Bostock House, is an ancient seat of the family of Lowndes, but is now occupied as a farm house. It has about one hundred and twenty-five acres of land attached to it, and belongs to the University of Cambridge, to which corporation it possibly passed from the Executors of the will of Thomas Lowndes. Most of the house is comparatively modern, but a portion of the front represents the original structure, and resembles the architecture of the time of Henry the Eighth. On the roof, under a canopy, is the bell which tolled the hours; the clock, which still exists, laid away in the garret, being affixed to the inside of the back wall of the central hall; the dial plate was on the outside of the back wall, and was, with the clock, removed only a few years since when alterations were made in the building. The front of the older portion of the building is covered with rough plaster or cement; the back shows the timbers filled in with mortar, so peculiar to ancient buildings in Cheshire. The walls of the modern portions of the building are of brick. A gateway built about 1700, with large stone posts, stands in front of the building.

† See also The Visitation of Chester in 1613.

WILLIAM³ LOWNDES above referred to, who married his cousin, Isabel Lawden, dau. of David or Daniel Lawden, and had issue. This William Lowndes, whose will was proved in October, 1592, had a son,

JOHN⁴ LOWNDES, who married Alice, daughter of Randall Rode, of Rode in Astbury, and had "a son and heir,

JOHN⁵ LOWNDES, aged 12, 1613," who married Alice Stephenson,* and had, with ten other children,

ROBERT⁶ LOWNDES, of Overton, who married Eleanor Raven, and was the father of

WILLIAM⁷ LOWNDES, of Overton and Lea, who married, on the 27th January, 1679–80, Elizabeth, daughter and eventually co-heir of Ralph⁴ Lowndes, of Lea Hall,† in Wimbaldsley, in the parish of Middlewich. The latter died in 1690, and left to his daughter the ancient residence of his family, in consequence of which William⁷ Lowndes established himself soon afterwards at Lea Hall. This gentleman is recorded in Burke as the founder of the present family of Lowndes of Barrington Hall. He resided sometimes at Overton and sometimes at Lea Hall, and was succeeded by his son,

JOHN⁸ LOWNDES, of Overton and Lea, who, by his wife Anne, had an only child,

SARAH,⁹ who married Awnsham Churchill, and had issue. She sold Lea and Overton to her uncles.

By the death of all the brothers of his mother without issue, Mr. Lowndes became heir to the estate of Lea Hall in accordance with the will of his uncle Ralph⁵ Lowndes of Lea, who died in 1716.

He was the brother of Thomas⁸ Lowndes, baptized at Astbury, Dec. 7, 1692, who was, according to Burke, the founder of the professorship of astronomy at Cambridge. He was also brother of

ROBERT⁸ LOWNDES,‡ who purchased the Lea estate from his niece Sarah, only child of John⁸ Lowndes of Overton and Lea, and who, by his first wife Ruth Graves, had :

i. ELIZABETH,⁹ who died, unmarried.

He married, 2dly, Mary, daughter of ——— Kenyon, and widow of the Rev. W. Turton, and by her had issue :

ii. EDWARD,⁹ of Charleston, South Carolina, who after a long residence in that city, returned to England, and died at 17 Mount Street, Westminster Road, in 1801, leaving an estate in Carolina.

* Burke.
† Lea Hall, in Wimbaldsley, in the parish of Middlewich, like many other old country houses in England is now occupied by a farmer; the present building, which occupies but a portion of the foundation of the original hall, is a large square house in the barbarous style of the Commonwealth period. Some of the walls about the grounds are still standing with their massive pillars. The parish church dates apparently from the end of the fifteenth century.

Ormerod, in his History of Cheshire, p. 101, says:

"There is a school in Middlewich, in which eight boys are educated free of expense, who are selected from the parish by the four church-wardens, each warden nominating two boys. This school was founded before 1693, when the parish had the appointment of the master; in 1709, R bert Lowndes nominated, who claimed that right on account of his giving the school-house. An indenture, dated June 24, 1762, recites that Ralph Lowndes, late of Lea Hall, Wimbaldsley, clerk, deceased, as owner of the mansion-house called Lea Hall, and the demesne lands thereto belonging, and of several other messuages, lands, tithes, hereditaments, in Lea, otherwise Wimbaldsley, in the parish of Middlewich, and elsewhere in the county of Chester, was entitled to the nomination of a master or masters of the school situate in Newton, near Middlewich, commonly called Middlewich School."

The manor of Wimbaldsley passed about the beginning of this century from the devisees of Robert Lowndes, Esq., to Sir Philip Leicester, Bart.

‡ Burke.

    iii. ROBERT,[9] of Lea and Palterton, who married Elizabeth, daughter and co-heir of Richard Milnes, of Chesterfield, and by her, who died in 1769, had:
        i. MILNES,[10] who died, *s. p.*, æt 36.
        ii. THOMAS,[10] of Barrington.
    iv. MARY.[9]

MARY[9] LOWNDES, who married Chadwick Gorst, Esq., of Preston, and died in 1804, had issue by him [who died in 1797]:

EDWARD[10] GORST, Esq., of Preston, who by Elizabeth, his wife, daughter of James Wigglesworth, Esq., had issue:
    i. THOMAS,[11] of Palterton, who took the name of Lowndes.
1.  ii. EDWARD-CHADDOCK,[11] who also assumed the name of Lowndes.
    iii. ELIZABETH.[11]
    iv. BARBARA-JANE.[11]
2.  v. MARY.[11]

1. EDWARD-CHADDOCK[11] LOWNDES, married Elizabeth, daughter of the late J. D. Nesham, Esq., and by her had issue. He died in 1859, and was succeeded by his elder son

EDWARD-CHADDOCK[12] LOWNDES, born in 1833, who was educated at Rugby and Trinity College, Cambridge; B.A. 1856, M.A. 1859. He is a magistrate for the counties of Lancaster and Wiltshire.

ARMS.—Argent, fretty azure on a canton, sable, a lion's head erased, or.
CREST.—A lion's head erased, or.
The arms, it will be noticed, are the same as those of Lowndes of Bostock, except in the color of the canton.
*Seats.*—Castle Combe, Chippenham.
        Palterton Hall, Mansfield.

2. MARY[11] GORST, of Preston, married in 1823, WILLIAM CLAYTON, Esq., of Lostock Hall, and had issue, among others:

GEORGE-ALAN[12] LOWNDES, Esq., of Barrington Hall, co. Essex; a Deputy Lieutenant and Justice of the Peace for that county, High Sheriff, 1861, who married Nov. 13, 1856, Helen-Emma, 2d daughter of the late Rev. Arthur-Johnson Daniell, of Rampisham Manor, co. Dorset, and has issue. Mr. Lowndes, whose patronymic is CLAYTON, assumed by royal license in 1840, the name and arms of LOWNDES in succeeding to the estate of the late Thomas Lowndes, Esq., of Barrington Hall.
*Seat.*—Barrington Hall, Halfield, Broad Oak, Essex.

---

The pedigree of the LOWNDES family of LEA HALL, sometimes written Legh Hall, was traced for the writer by the late Mr. H. G. Somerby, from

ROGER[1] LOWNDES, of Sandbach, who, in accordance with a request in his will, was buried in the church there on the 17th of May, 1586. By his wife, Ellen, he had a son,

RALPH,[2] born before 1562, who married, October 22, 1587, Elizabeth Poole, and had

RALPH[3] LOWNDES, who married, May 21, 1622, Eleanor Lea, and was the father of

SAMUEL[4] LOWNDES, of Marshall, and

RALPH[4] LOWNDES, of Lea Hall, gent., baptized May 21, 1626, who m. Elizabeth ———, and d. in 1690, having made his will Jan. 26, 1688-9. He was the father, among others, of

i. RALPH,⁵ bapt. at Middlewich, Oct. 29, 1663, who bequeathed Lea Hall to his nephew, John⁸ Lowndes, of Overton, son of his sister Elizabeth. He made his will July 12, 1716, but it was not proved till Sept. 22, 1727.
ii. THOMAS,⁵ who was named in his father's will as entitled to a bequest when he should attain the age of twenty-one, of whom presently.
iii. ELIZABETH,⁵ who was married at Middlewich on the 27th of January, 1679–80, to William Lowndes, of Overton, as has been already mentioned.

THOMAS⁵ LOWNDES, who was not of age in 1689, and who probably died unmarried, is often confused with his nephew, Thomas⁸ of Overton, born in 1692.

It is somewhat difficult to determine which of these two persons, uncle and nephew, was Provost Marshal of South Carolina and also the founder of the professorship at Cambridge, as is manifest from the provisions of the will containing the bequest. Burke has accepted without question, in his account of the Barrington Hall family, the claim of that line. Yet a study of the probabilities of the case, and of the pedigree of the Lea Hall family, would point to the older wearer of the name as the bustling and nervous correspondent of the Board of Trade a hundred and fifty years ago.

Thomas Lowndes, who described himself as of Overton in the county of Chester, residing in London, made his will May 6, 1748, and died shortly after. In his will, which was proved on the 4th of June following, he directed his lands in Smallwood and other places in Cheshire to be sold, and the proceeds devoted to the foundation of a professorship of astronomy at Cambridge. He left also bequests to the University of Oxford, and to the Foundling Hospital. He bequeathed his baronies of land in South Carolina to Randle Wilbraham, Esq., and Thomas Booth, Esq., in trust, they to have out of them £100 each. He also spoke of his invention relative to salt. His will, however, contains no mention of any of his kindred, and is therefore of no help in a direct determination of his family. Of the first named of his executors, Thomas Booth, little is known. The second, Randle Wilbraham, was of Rode, in Cheshire; he was a barrister-at-law, LL.D. and Deputy Steward of the University of Oxford.

It is clear that the signer of this will was the same Thomas Lowndes who was Provost Marshal of Carolina under the Lords Proprietors, and again under the Crown. By the records of the Board of Trade for October 25, 1726, there is entered a grant of twelve thousand acres of land in South Carolina to Isaac Lowndes, his heirs and assigns, who, by a deed of the 26th of August, 1729, declared that his name was made use of only as trustee for Thomas Lowndes, of the city of Westminster, gent. And this Isaac Lowndes was a son of Samuel⁴ Lowndes, of Marshall, and therefore first cousin to Thomas⁵ Lowndes, of Lea, the elder of the name. It would seem to be more probable, that Isaac⁵ should have held the trusteeship for his cousin than for a more distant relative. Nor is there any improbability that Thomas,⁵ of Lea, should have, late in life, purchased Overton, when that estate was sold by the heiress, Sarah, daughter of John⁸ Lowndes, since his elder sister Elizabeth, by her marriage with William Lowndes of Overton, had lived and died there.

If, on the other hand, we accept Burke's statement that the founder of the Cambridge professorship was Thomas the younger, son of Elizabeth, we are driven to the conclusion that he was hardly thirty-two years of age, when, after long scheming over the settlement of the Carolinas, he received the Patents of Provost Marshal, Clerk of the Peace and Clerk of the Crown, and carried on a correspondence with the Board of Trade, the whole tone of which shows that he was of age and experience, although somewhat of an invalid, and given to persistent and worrying complaints.*

There remains, in conclusion, but one other family to notice. It is, however, of unusual interest, since it is that with which the American families of the name in Virginia, and possibly in Maryland, claim descent. For the following statement of pedigree showing its several branches, each of which has now for more than a century and a half constituted a separate county family, the writer is indebted to the compilation from the family papers in possession of William Lowndes. Esquire, of the Bury, Chesham, Bucks.†

Captain ——[1] LOWNES, who was believed to be a son of Robert[1] Lowndes of Winslow, by Jane Croke, or Crowke, his wife, and who was an early settler of Virginia, where he acquired a large plantation, by his will settled his estates on his heirs male, with remainder to the heirs male of the younger son of William Lowndes, of Winslow, co. Bucks. He m. Anne, daughter and heiress of ——— Gates, of Jamestown, of the family of Sir Thomas Gates.‡ by whom he had issue:—

    i. WILLIAM,[2] who died in 1589.
1. ii. ROBERT,[2] born 1591.
    iii. SARAH,[2] born 1596.

1. ROBERT[2] LOWNES, who lived at Jamestown from 1620 to 1650, m. Elizabeth Newport, and had :—

    i. RICHARD,[3] died young, 1631.
    ii. JOHN,[3] died in infancy, 1622.
2. iii. WILLIAM,[3] born 1624.

2. WILLIAM[3] LOWNES, m. in 1650, Anne Brocas, and had :—

3. i. JOHN,[4] born 1654.
4. ii. ROBERT,[4] born 1656.
    iii. REBECCA,[4] died in infancy.

3. JOHN[4] LOWNES, of Jamestown and Lownes Creek, in Virginia, merchant and planter. m. Margaret,[4] daughter of Robert[3] Lowndes, of Winslow, co. Bucks, by whom he had :—

---

\* Records of the Board of Trade, Colonial Papers, Carolina 2, Vol. 5. (See Appendix.)

† This gentleman, who is Lord of the Manor of Chesham, is also the owner of the adjoining estate of Hundrich, in Chesham, which was held by the Chase family of that place for nearly two centuries from the time of Henry the 7th, when a younger branch of the Suffolk family of that name moved into Buckinghamshire, and settled at Chesham, Amersham and Great Marlow. From a younger son of a junior branch of the Chase family of Chesham, descends the large American family which settled in Essex County, Massachusetts, about 1636, and has spread from that county over a large part of New-England and the north-western States.—See "Heraldic Journal," vol. iv. 1868; Art "Chase Family."

‡ Sir Thomas Gates was a member of the London Company, formed in 1609 for the colonization of Virginia. He sailed, with Sir George Summers, soon after, but was wrecked near the Bermudas, and did not reach Jamestown til the following year, six months after Captain Smith had left it. Finding it in a starving condition, he embarked with the remaining settlers, about sixty in all, for Newfoundland. At the mouth of the river they encountered Lord De la War, the new Governor, "with provisions and comforts of all kinds," and returned with him to Jamestown. In 1611, when Lord De la War resigned his office, Sir Thomas Gates, who had previously returned to England, was appointed by the Council to succeed him, with full powers as Governor.—*Old Churches, Ministers, and Families of Virginia. Bishop Meade*, i. pp. 69, 75, et supra.

  i. Robert,⁵ of Jamestown and Lownes Creek, in Virginia, born 1692; died in 1775, *s.p.*, when the settled estates passed to his uncle's grandson as heir male. He left his personal estate to Charles Lownes, of ———.
  ii. Margaret,⁵ married James Baez.
  iii. Rebecca,⁵ died in childhood.
  iv. Anne,⁵ died in childhood.
  v. James,⁵ died in childhood.

4. Robert⁴ Lownes, of Jamestown, married Mary Jennings, and had by her :—
 5. i. William,⁵ born 1697.
  ii. Anne,⁵ died young.
  iii. Mary,⁵ " "
  iv. Sarah,⁵ " "
  v. Robert,⁵ " "

5. William⁵ Lownes, of Matovey Creek, married, in 1757, Jane Wormley, and had by her :—
  i. Richard,⁶ born 1757, who succeeded to the settled estates in Virginia, when he was eighteen years of age, and who died in 1830, unmarried.
  ii. Mary,⁶ m. ——— Lee, of Jamestown.

Robert¹ Lowndes, of Winslow, a scion of the ancient family of Lowndes, of Lea Hall, in Buckinghamshire, who died in 1602, married in 1576 Jane Croke, or Crowke, and had, among other children,
William² Lowndes, of Winslow, bapt. Jan. 5, 1585, upon whose children the American estates with remainder were settled, in accordance with the will of Captain ———¹ Lownes, died in James City, June 6, 1654. He m. Oct. 27, 1612, Frances Wendover, and had twelve children, of whom we notice :—
  i. Edmund,³ bapt. 1617, who lived in Virginia and North Carolina, from 1643 to 1650. In 1650, he discharged certain trusts as Trustee to the settled estates with Robert² Lownes, at James City, on the marriage of William³ Lownes and Anne Brocas.
 1. ii. Robert,³ bapt. July 4, 1619.

1. Robert³ Lowndes, of Winslow, who fled to America in 1642, where he remained for about eight years, when he returned to Winslow, and there resided till his death. He was buried Jan. 29, 1683. He married 1st, Margaret Selby, and had :—
  i. Margaret,⁴ wife of John Lownes of Jamestown.

Mr. Lowndes married 2d, Elizabeth, daughter of Peter Fitzwilliam, and had, with four daughters, a son :—
  William⁴ Lowndes,* of Westminster, and of Winslow, born at Winslow, Nov. 1, 1652.

This gentleman, who has already been referred to, was by far the most distinguished man of all who have ever borne, in England, his old and well-known name. He sat for many years in the House of Commons, and served as Chairman of the Committee of Ways and Means. He originated the funding system, and rose to great power and influence in Parliament. In recognition of his services, Queen Anne conferred upon him the office of auditor of the land revenue for life, in reversion to his sons, with an augmentation to his coat of arms. He married 1st, Oct. 24, 1677, Elizabeth,

* Dictionary of the Landed Gentry. Sir Bernard Burke. Art. Lowndes of Whaddon.

daughter of Sir Roger Harsnett, and by her, who died Nov. 6, 1680, had a son :—

    2. i. ROBERT,[5] his heir; bapt. in 1678, at Winslow.

Mr. Lowndes married 2d, Nov. 26, 1683, Jane Hopper, by whom, who died in July, 1685, he had a daughter :—

    ii. ANNE,[5] born in 1684, who married.

Mr. Lowndes married 3d, Jan. 12, 1686, Elizabeth, daughter of the Rev. Richard Martyn, D.D., by whom, who died July 6, 1689, he had :—

    3. iii. WILLIAM,[5] of Astwood Bury, ancestor of the family of LOWNDES-STONE, of Brightonwell Park.
    iv. ELIZABETH,[5] born in 1688; m. Thomas Duncombe, Esq., and d. in 1712.

Mr. Lowndes married 4th, Nov. 29, 1691, Rebecca, daughter of John Shales, by whom he had fourteen children, seven sons and seven daughters, and among them,

    4. CHARLES[6] LOWNDES, ancestor of the family of LOWNDES of *Chesham.*

Mr. Lowndes died in 1722. In his will, dated March 27, 1721-2, proved 1723, he desired to be buried at Winslow, co. Bucks, where he was born. He also mentioned his eldest son Robert and his sons Richard, Joseph and William. To his eldest son by his "present wife" he bequeathed the new house at Chesham, and entailed his property, which was very large, upon his grandchildren.

Mr. Lowndes was succeeded by his son,

    2. ROBERT[5] LOWNDES,* Esquire, of Winslow, Bucks, who died in 1728, and left by his wife Margaret, a son and his successor,

RICHARD[6] LOWNDES, Esquire, of Winslow, high sheriff of Bucks in 1742, and M. P. for that county in the same year. He married Essex, youngest daughter and co-heir of Charles Shales, of London, by Anne, his wife, 2nd daughter and co-heir of Thomas Barrington, Esq., son of Sir John Barrington, Bart., of Barrington Hall, who was 3rd in descent from the marriage of Sir Thomas Barrington with the Honorable Winifred Pole, granddaughter and co-heir of Margaret Plantagenet, Countess of Salisbury, daughter and sole heir of George, Duke of Clarence, brother of King Edward IV.

By this lady, Mr. Lowndes left a son and successor,

WILLIAM[7] LOWNDES, of Winslow and Whaddon, who took the name of Selby before Lowndes. By his wife Mary, daughter of Thomas Goostrey, Esq., of London, whom he married in 1766, he had :

    i. WILLIAM,[8] his heir.
    ii. ROBERT.[8]
    iii. RICHARD,[8] A.M., Vicar of Swanbourne.
    iv. THOMAS,[8] LL.B., Rector of North Crawley.

WILLIAM-SELBY[8] LOWNDES, Esq., of Whaddon Hall and Winslow, who sat in Parliament as member for Buckinghamshire from 1807 to 1820, married Aug. 25, 1806, Ann-Eleanora-Isabella, daughter of the Rev. Graham Hanmer, and had issue :

    i. WILLIAM-SELBY,[9] his heir, born Nov. 5, 1807.
    ii. THOMAS-WILLIAM,[9] b. Oct. 8, 1810.
    iii. RICHARD-WILLIAM,[9] b. Oct. 2, 1811.
    iv. HARRY-WILLIAM,[9] b. Sept. 20, 1812.
    v. EDWARD-WILLIAM,[9] b. Sept. 9, 1813.
    vi. CHARLES-WILLIAM,[9] b. Nov. 10, 1815.

* Burke.

Mr. Selby Lowndes died May 18, 1840, and was succeeded by WILLIAM-SELBY⁹ LOWNDES, now of Whaddon Hall and Winslow, co. Bucks, who married, first, June 28, 1832, Lucy, eldest daughter of Isaac-Rawlings Hartman, Esq., Coldstream Guards, and by her, who died 21st October, 1852, has issue.

Mr. Lowndes married, second, Clara, 2d dau. of I.-R. Hartman, Esq.

Mr. Selby Lowndes is one of the co-heirs of the Barony of Grandison, and also a co-heir of the Barony of Montacute. He has petitioned her majesty to determine the abeyance of the latter in his favor.

Arms of Lowndes of Whaddon: Argent fretty azure, the interlacing each charged with a bezant, on a canton, gules, a leopard's head erased at the neck, or. Crest, a leopard's head, as in the arms, gorged with a laurel branch, ppr.

Seat, Whaddon Hall, Winslow, Bucks.

3. WILLIAM⁵ LOWNDES,* of ASTWOOD BURY, in Bucks, grandson of Robert³ Lowndes, the Virginia refugee, married in 1711, Margaret, daughter and heiress of —— Layton, Esquire, and had issue:

WILLIAM,⁶ born in 1712, who married, 1744, Catherine, eldest daughter of Francis Lowe, Esq., of Baldwyn Brightwell, in the County of Oxford, and assumed, in consequence of the testamentary injunction of Mr. Lowe, the surname of STONE. He died in 1773, and left, with a daughter Catherine, a son, who became

WILLIAM⁷ LOWNDES, of Astwood and North Crawley, Bucks, and of Baldwyn Brightwell, co. Oxford. He was born in 1750, and on the death of his mother in 1789, assumed the surname and arms of STONE. He married, in 1775, Elizabeth, 2d daughter and co-heir of Richard Garth, Esquire, of Morden, in Surrey, and by her, who died in 1837, had with five daughters, three sons:

 i. WILLIAM-FRANCIS.⁸
 ii. RICHARD,⁸ born in 1790, in holy orders, who assumed the surname of Garth.
 iii. HENRY-OWEN,⁸ born in 1795, who settled in America, and married in 1827, Sarah-Anne, daughter of Augustus Trimbish, Esq., and had issue.

William-Francis⁸ Lowndes-Stone, b. Oct. 27, 1783; married, October 3, 1811, Caroline, 2d daughter of Sir William Strickland, Bart., of Boynton, co. York, and had, among others,

 WILLIAM-CHARLES,⁹ b. Aug. 7, 1812, who married, May 7, 1840, Catherine, daughter of Rev. Reginald Winniatt, and by her left at his decease, April 21, 1845, two daughters:
  i. CATHERINE CHARLOTTE.¹⁰
  ii. SUSAN.¹⁰

CATHERINE CHARLOTTE¹⁰ succeeded her grandfather on his death, in 1858, and married in 1862, her cousin, Capt. Robert Thomas Norton of the Grenadier Guards, by whom she has issue:

 i. ——, a son, born 1863.

Seat, Brightwell Park, Tetsworth, Oxfordshire.†

* Dictionary of the Landed Gentry.
† For description of Brightwell Park, see Burke's Visitation of Seats and Arms, ii. p. 196.

4. CHARLES⁵ LOWNDES,* son of William Lowndes, Esq., Secretary of the Treasury, by his fourth wife, Rebecca Shales, married Anne, eldest daughter and co-heir of Charles Shales, and sister of Essex Shales, who married Richard Lowndes, nephew of Charles. By this lady Mr. Secretary Lowndes had

WILLIAM⁶ LOWNDES, of Chesham, Commissioner of Excise, who married Lydia Mary, daughter of Robert Osborne, Esq., and had a son and successor,

WILLIAM⁷ LOWNDES, Esq., of Chesham, who married Harriet, daughter of John Kingston, of Rickmansworth, Herts, and left issue, with seven other children,

WILLIAM⁸ LOWNDES, Esq., of Chesham, who died in 1864; a Justice of the Peace for Bucks and Herts; Deputy Lieutenant for the former county and High Sheriff in 1848; a B. C. L. of Trinity Hall, Cambridge, who was born Nov. 24, 1807, and married twice. By his first wife Mary Harriet, daughter of Kender Mason, Esq., of Bell House, Amersham, who died April 18, 1836, he had,

WILLIAM⁹ LOWNDES, Esq., of the Bury, Chesham; who has been already referred to as the furnisher for this memoir of the Virginia pedigree above given. Mr. Lowndes, who was born in 1834, was educated at Trinity Hall, Cambridge, and received the degree of LL.B. in 1863. He was called to the bar, at Lincoln's Inn, in 1859. He is a Justice of the Peace and Deputy Lieutenant for Buckinghamshire.

Mr. Lowndes, who is a claimant of the ancient Barony of Monthermer, quarters the arms of Lowndes of Winslow, with those of Shales, Barrington, Pole, and Plantagenet. The crest is the same as Lowndes of Whaddon. His motto is "Ways and Means."

Seat, The Bury, Chesham.

The earliest seats in Cheshire of the Lowndes family, who received a grant of arms in 1180, were at Orton and at Lea Hall. A branch settled at a very early period in the county of York, the name of Lownde of Cave, of Holdernesse, of Thorneton in the Benes, and of Harewood continually occurring in the commissions of array for that county in the 13th and 14th centuries.

William⁷ Lowndes, of the Bury, Chesham, made during his life-time extensive collections of documents relating to the several families of Lowndes. According to the old pedigree of the Winslow branch, the first of the name in England, and the common ancestor of the race, was William, Seigneur de Lounde, who accompanied William the Conqueror into England in 1066, and acquired large possessions in the counties of Bucks, Northampton, Lincoln and Bedford. From him Robert¹ Lowndes of Winslow, who married Jane Coiks, Croke, or Crowke, as the name has been variously spelled, was sixteenth in descent. It is not improbable that this pedigree is correct, yet it should be, like all ancestral records which come down to us from so remote a period, regarded only as a possible or probable pedigree. Indeed, there are few family records in England which spring from the Conquest, except those of great historic lines, closely interwoven with that of the times in which they lived, that can be regarded as wholly correct.

* Burke's Dictionary of the Landed Gentry.

A pedigree of the family of Perchay is recorded in the Herald's Visitations of Yorkshire, 1584–1612, which shows also the antiquity of the family of Lownde and their arms. Thomas or John Perchay, who lived about 1350, married a daughter and heir of Lownde of Riton, in Risdale, whose arms are quartered with those of Perchay, and are the same, argent fretty azure, as Lowndes of Bostock, but without the canton.

Bardsley, in his work on surnames, derives the name of Lowndes from the old English word of launde, which "signified a pretty and rich piece of grassy sward in the heart of a forest, what we should now call an open wood, in fact. Thus it is we term the space in our gardens within the surrounding shrubberies, *lawns*.

" Chaucer says of Theseus on hunting bent—
> To the *launde* he rideth him ful right,
> There was the hart wont to have his flight.

"In the 'Morte Arthur,' too, we are told of hunting—
> At the hartes in these hye *laundes*.

"This is the source of more surnames than we might imagine.
" Hence are sprung our 'Launds,' 'Lands,' 'Lowndes,'"* etc.

In a list of ninety-nine wills of persons of this name proved, in the probate court at Chester, between the years 1586 and 1768, the writer found the names variously spelled, viz.: Lounds, Lownes, Lounde, Loundes, Lound, Lownde, Lownds, Lowndes. The first of the spellings here given occurs in the will of Roger Lounds of Sandbach, and the last, which has been the form in general use for now more than a century, is found in that of John Lowndes of Cranage.

---

NOTES contributed to the local column of the Manchester (England) Courier:—

NOTE No. 238.—" On the 5th of June, 1830, died at the Hot Wells, Bristol, in his 86th year, Robert Lowndes, Esq., formerly of Lea Hall, Cheshire, and of Chesterfield, Derby, but late of Widcombe Crescent, Bath. He was the eldest male representative of the Lowndes of Overton Hall, from whom are descended the Lowndes of Buckinghamshire and Oxfordshire."

This gentleman was undoubtedly Robert[9] Lowndes. (See p. 46.)

NOTE No. 313.—" Robert Lowndes of Rochdale, attorney-at-law, was appointed by Lord Byron Steward of the Manor, and held his first cause there, 2 May, 1723. The old Manorial Rolls from this date ceased to be in Latin, and the entries are made in books, in English. Mr. Lowndes made his last cause 23d May, 1747. He married at Rochdale Church, 19th June, 1726, Ruth, daughter of William Greaves of Gartside Hall, Gent., and sister of William Greaves, Esq., Fellow of Clare Hall, and Commissary of the University of Cambridge, who assumed on his marriage the additional names of Beaupre-Bell."

* "Our English Surnames," by Charles Wareing Bardsley, M.A.

# APPENDIX.

## PART I.

### ABSTRACTS OF DEEDS, WILLS, &c.

#### ( 1 )

##### EXTRACTED FROM CONGLETON BOROUGH DEEDS [p. 11].

Indenture made 20th October 23. Charles 1st 1648. between Edmund Spencer of Longe Eaton in the County of Derby Gent of the one Part, and *Richard Lowndes* of Bostock House in the County of Chester Gentleman of the other Part, Being a Feoffment to the said Richard Lowndes his heirs & assigns for ever of a Messuage and Tenement with the appurtenances commonly called the Kings Head situated in Hegle Street in Congleton in the said County of Chester together with a moss room upon Mossley Moss in Congleton aforesaid & two sittings in Congleton Chapell.

Indenture made 13. Oct$^r$. 1657. between John Lowndes of Middlewich of the one part and William Welde of Newbold Astbury Gent and John Welde of London Gent of the other part being a feoffment to the said John & William Welde & their Heirs of the above premises upon trust to the use of the said John Lowndes during his natural life Remainder to John Lowndes second son of the said John Lowndes & his heirs, Remainder to Christopher Lowndes third son of the s$^d$. John Lowndes & his heirs remainder to Edward Lowndes the fourth son & his heirs & remainder to the right heirs of John Lowndes.

Indent. 29 & 30 May 36 Cha$^s$. II. Release from John Lowndes of Clerkenwell gent. William Welde and John Welde & Rich$^d$ Lowndes of Bostock house to W$^m$ Dean of Congleton, of the above premises.

#### ( 2 )

##### WILL OF FRANCES' LOWNDES, OF COVENT GARDEN [p. 11].

In the Name of God Amen I ffrances Lowndes of the Parish of S$^t$. Paul Covent Garden in the County of Midd$^x$ Spinster being infirme of body but of good and perfect memory all praise be therefore given unto Allmighty God and calling to mind the fraile and uncertaine Condicōn of this Transitory Life doe make and ordaine this my Last Will and Testament in manner and forme following (that is to say) first and principally I commend my Soule into the hands of Allmighty God my Creator trusting and assuredly hopeing through the merritts and mediacon of my blessed Lord and Saviour Jesus Christ to inheritt Eternall life my body I committ to the Earth whence twas extracted to bee decently buried in Christian Buriall at the discretion of my Executors hereinafter named in sure and certaine Expectation of A Joyfull Resurrectione at the Last day And in respect of my worldly Estate wherewith it hath pleased Allmighty God to bless mee I order and dispose of the same as followeth (viz$^t$) Imp$^r$is I give and bequeath unto my brother in Law John Walker A debt of Twenty pounds which is due and oweing to mee upon bond from my brother Richard Lowndes Gent and the said bond and all Interest and other profitts due and accruing due thereupon In Trust neverthelesse to and for the only proper use and behoofe of my Neice ffrances Binet daughter of my brother in Law Robert Binet the summe of Twenty pounds sterl' to bee paid to or taken by the said Robert Binet in trust for his said daughter untill shee shall have attained to her Age of one and Twenty yeares or day of Marriage (which shall first happen) Item I give and bequeath unto my Nephew Charles Lowndes sonn of my brother Charles Lowndes the summe of Tenne pounds sterl. to bee paid to or taken by my said brother Charles Lowndes in trust for his said sonn vntill hee shall have attained to his Age of one and Twenty yeares. Item I give and bequeath unto my Mother Jane Lowndes and to my Sister Elianor Binet and to my Sister in Law Sarah Lowndes wife of my said brother Charles Lowndes and to my brother in Law John Walker and my sister Awdrey his wife and to my sister Mary Savill and to M$^{rs}$ Simpson and to M$^{rs}$ Price and to Madam Elizabeth Brereton and to my Cozen Anne Whittingham a Ring of Tenn Shillings price a peece Item I give and bequeath unto M$^r$. Sebastian Jason Two Guines to buy him A Ring Item I give and bequeath unto the Lady Harriett Churchill and to the Lady Ann Churchill a ring of five shillings price a peece The rest and residue of all and singular my estate ready money plate goods and Chattells whatsoever (my debts Legacies and funerall expences being thereout first defaulked paid and discharged) I give and bequeath unto my said brother Charles Lowndes and my said brother in Law Robert Binet equally to bee divided betweene them part and share like whome I doe hereby make and appoint joynt Executors of this my Last Will and Testament And I doe hereby annihilate renounce and make void all former Wills and Testaments by mee made declareing this present Testament to bee my true and last Will In Wittnesse whereof I have hereunto sett my hand and seale the Seaven and Twentieth day of March Anno Dño 1690 And in the second yeare of the Reigne of their Maj$^{ties}$ King William and Queene Mary &c.

FRANCES LOWNDES.

Seald Subscribed published and declared by the Testatrix ffrances Lowndes as and for her last Will and Testament in the p'sence of us who have hereunto Attested the same as Wittnesses thereto in her presence.

William Ellis  William Hues  Rob$^t$. Hodson.

Probatum apud London fuit humoi Testum Coram venli viro Dño Thoma Pinfold mite Legum deore Surro veñlis et egregii viri Dñi Richi Raines Militis Legum etiam deoris Curiæ Prærogat Cantuar Magri Custodis sive

Comq ltime constituti Vndecimo die mensis Aprilis Anno Dñi Millimo Sexccñmo Nonagemo Juram Caroli Lowndes et Robti Binett Exrūm in deo Testamᵗᵒ nominat Quibus comissa fuit Admico omniū et singulorū bonorū juriū et cred dict deft de bene et fidelr Admistrando eadem ad Sancta Dei Evangelia Jurat. Examʳ.
Prerog. Court of Cantʸ. Doctors Commons.
Dyke 60.

NOTE.—The name of Frances Lowndes does not occur in any of the Registers of St. Paul's, Covent Garden. She could not therefore have been long a resident of that parish. She probably came to London a short time before her death, took apartments in Covent Garden, at that time the fashionable quarter of the town, and was taken ill soon after.

( 3 )

## WILL OF JANE LOWNDES, OF CHECKLEY, WIDOW.

In the name of God amen the fifteenth day of July and in the yeare of our Lord God one thousand six hundred and ninetye I Jane Lowndes of Checkley in the County of Chester widdow being by divers infirmities put in mind of my mortalitye knowinge that death is certaine but the hour thereof most uncertaine doe in perfect memory make this my last will and Testament in writinge in manner and forme followinge And first I Commend my soule into the hands of the Almighty God my Creator hopeinge and faithfully beleivinge that all my sins are purged and done away in and throughe the blood of my blessed Saviour Jesus Christ And that I shall arise againe an incorruptable body to Raigne with him in his blessed Kingdome for ever And my body I commend to the earth to bee decently buried by my Ex'ors hereafter named And for those worldly goods wherewith God hath blessed mee I do hereby dispose of the same in manner and forme following And first my will and pleasure is and I doe hereby give and bequeath unto my grandchild *John Walker* the clerke 44 yerds of new flaxen cloth one dozen of new napkins 4½ yards of new towells the broad piece of gold and four gold rings And if it shall happen that my said grandchild shall die and depart this life before he come to the age of 21 years Then my will and pleasure is that my grandchild *William Walker* shall have all the gifts and bequests that are now given to his brother *John Walker*. Also I doe hereby give and bequeath unto my daughter *Mary Swile* one shilling Also I doe give and bequeath unto my daughter *Ellen Bennett* 2/6. Also I doe hereby give and bequeath unto my son *Richard Lowndes* one pound Also unto my son *Charles Lowndes* 2/6. Also I give and bequeath unto Margaret Cocke one flanell peticote, one sagg peticote and all my shoos. Also I doe hereby give and bequeath unto my sister Anne Welde my last Holland Showes. Also I doe hereby give and bequeath all the rest and the remainder of my apparill unto my daughter Awdry Walker. And my will and pleasure is and I doe hereby order appoynte and Alott the sume of £20 for my funerall charge and expences. And lastly I doe hereby give and bequeath all the rest and remainder of all my goods to my grandchild John Walker if he shall attain to the years of 21 and if not then to his brother William Walker. And I doe hereby constitute ordaine and make my Loveing brother Mʳ William Welde of

Little Hassall my sole executor to see this my last will and Testament executed and performed according to the trust I repose in him. And I doe hereby adnull and revoke all former and other will or wills by me heretofore made and doe pronounce this my last will and Testament And in witnesse hereof I have hereunto put my hand and seale the day and yeare first above written.
JANE LOWNDES.

Mary Welde  
Anne Welde  
Mary Whittingham  
y<sup>e</sup> marke of John Johnson  
} Witnesses.

proved 12 May 1691.

A true and perfect Inventory of all and singuler the goods and Creditts of M<sup>rs</sup> Jane Lowndes deceased Taken and appraised by John Walker senior and John Walker junior at Checkley the 8<sup>th</sup> of March Annoq dñi 1690.

|  | £ | s. | d. |
|---|---|---|---|
| Imprmis the Clocke | 02 | 10 | 00 |
| Item 44 yards of new flaxen cloth | 02 | 10 | 00 |
| Item one dozen of napkins | 00 | 12 | 00 |
| Item 4 yards and ½ of new Toweling | 00 | 04 | 06 |
| Item 4 gold rings and one broad piece of gold | 02 | 13 | 00 |
| Item moneys in her purse | 11 | 18 | 00 |
| Item moneys oweinge her | 22 | 10 | 00 |
| Item Desperate Debts | 15 | 00 | 00 |
| Item more moneys oweing | 01 | 16 | 04 |
| Item her weareing clothes and Linnen | 10 | 00 | 00 |
| Item her Bookes | 00 | 10 | 00 |
| Item some Boxes and small thinges forgott | 00 | 02 | 00 |
|  | 70 | 05 | 10 |

In witness &c.  
John Walker  
John Walker    Exhibited, 12 May 1691

( 4 )

WILL OF WILLIAM WELD OF HASSALL, 1699.

In the name of God Amen. I William Weld of Little Hassall in the parish of Sandbach in the County of Chester gentleman doe make this my last Will and Testament this Twelfth day of September in the year of our Lord One thousand six hundred and ninety nine And first I doe hereby give and devise unto my loveing wife Mary Weld and her assigns all my Messuages lands tenem<sup>ts</sup> hereditaments tithes and leasehold lands with their and every of their appurteñces lying & being in Hassall Newbold Astbury and Congleton in the said County of Chester or any of them for and dureing her naturall life if she keep herselfe sole and unmarried I likewise give and bequeath unto her all my personall estate goods and Chattells whatsoever And from and after the death of the said Mary my wife I hereby give and bequeath all my said Messuages lands tenem<sup>ts</sup> and hereditamts wherein I have any Estate of Inheritance in possession reversion or remainder to Richard Lowndes the younger of Hassall aforesaid son and heir of Richard Lowndes my Nephew And I doe hereby further give and devise unto my sister Ann Weld my Nephew M$^r$ Thomas Whittingham Rector of Brereton my Nephew William Whittingham my niece Ann Whittingham Elizabeth Whittingham daughter to William Whittingham to my Nephew Charles Lowndes the elder to his brother William Lowndes my Godson to my Godson William Walker to John Lowndes brother of the said Richard Lowndes and to Richard Lowndes the elder father of the said Richard Lowndes the young$^r$ the severall yearly sumes herein after mentioned to be issuing and goeing out of all my said Messuages lands and premises and payable to them respectively for and during their respective natural lives at two dayes of payment that is to say upon the nine and twentieth day of September and the five and twentieth day of March yearly by equall portions the first payment to be made at such of the said dayes as shall first happen next after the death of my said wife which said yearly sumes are these herein after following that is to say to my said sister Ann Weld ten pounds to the said Thomas Whittingham Rector of Brereton ten pounds to my said nephew William Whittingham five pounds to my said niece Ann Whittingham five pounds if she doe not marry John Swaine To the said Elizabeth Whittingham daughter to William Whittingham five pounds to the said Charles Lowndes the elder five pounds to the said William Lowndes my godson five pounds to the said William Walker my godson five pounds to the said John Lowndes five pounds to the said Richard Lowndes the elder father of the said Richard Lowndes the younger five pounds all which said several yearly summs I give unto them severally and respectively with power to distrayne for nonpayment as in case of a rent charge. I hereby further give and bequeath to every servant of mine that shall be with me at the time of my death forty shillings apiece and to the poore of the parish of Sandbach twenty pounds to be equally distributed amongst them And I doe hereby constitute and appoint my said loveing wife Executrix and the said Richard Lowndes Executor of this my last Will and Testament In witness whereof I have hereunto sett my hand and seal the day and year first above written.

WILL { L. S. } WELD

Signed sealed and published in the presence of
    G Booth
    Mary Booth
    Peter Brittain

# PART II.

### DOCUMENTS

*Relating to South Carolina, with Letters from Thomas Lowndes and others, filed among the Colonial Papers, Record Office, London.*

( 1 )

[ENDORSEMENT.]—Grant to M$^r$ Tho: Lowndes of 12000 Acres of land in S$^{th}$ Carolina dated y$^e$ 25$^{th}$ Oct. 1726.

To all to whom these presents shall come:

His Excellency John Lord Carteret, Palatine; the most Noble Henry Duke of Beaufort, y$^e$ Right Hon$^{ble}$ William Lord Craven, y$^e$ Hon$^{ble}$ James Ber... & Henry Bertie his brother, Sir John Colleton Bar$^t$ & Sir John Ty... ll Bar$^t$, being seven of the eight true and absolute Lords Proprietors of ...olina, send greeting. Whereas *Tho: Lowndes* hath surrendered to us, ... heirs & Assigns a Grant for four Baronies in our Province of Caro.... ; containing in the whole Forty-eight Thousand Acres of Land, toge.... with the Title, Dignity & Honour of a Landgrave, w$^{ch}$ was heretofore granted to John Price Gent: In consideration whereof we do Consent & Agree to grant to the said *Tho: Lowndes* one Tract or Barony of Land to contain Twelve Thousand Acres of Land. One other such like Tract or Barony of Land to *Isaac Lowndes*; one other such like Tract or Barony of Land to *Cha$^s$ Edwards Gent*: & one other such like Tract or Barony of Land to *John Beresford Gent*: all which four Baronies are to contain in the whole Forty-eight Thousand Acres of Land, to the end and intent that he & they, & his & their Heirs & Assigns may hold & enjoy the same (according to their several & respective Grants) together with all such Liberties, Benefits, Immunities, Priviledges & Advantages whatsoever as we have power to grant by Virtue of the Letters Patents Granted to our Ancestors or Predecessors. Now these Presents Witness, That We, the said Lords Proprietors, in Consideration of the Premises, Have given & granted & by these Presents do Give & Grant unto the said Tho: Lowndes, his heirs & Assigns one Barony or Tract of Land to contain Twelve Thousand Acres of Land, together with all the Wood, Timber, Royalties & Advantages to be had, found, received & taken thereby, & all our Estate, Inheritance, Use, Possession, Claim & Demand of Us the s$^d$ Lords Proprietors, of, in, to or out of the same Premises hereby given & granted with their Appurtenances, unto the said Tho: Lowndes, his Heirs & Assigns, unto the only use of y$^e$ s$^d$ Tho: Lowndes, his Heirs & Assigns for ever, Yielding & Paying to the s$^d$ Lords Proprietors, their Heirs & Assigns for ever the Summ of One Penny Sterling Yearly at the Royal Exchange of London on the feast of St. Michael the Archangel for ever.

Provided nevertheless that in case this present Grant shall not be duly inrolled within the space of Two Years after the Date hereof in one of his Majesty's Courts of Record at Westminster, or in the office of the proper Register, Secretary, or in the Inrollment Office of the said Province; Then this present grant shall be void & of none effect. And the said Lords

Proprietors do hereby authorize and require that the Surveyor Gen¹ of the Province of South Carolina immediately, within 20 days after notice given him of this present Grant, do allot & set out the said Tract or Barony of Land in any Place within the said Province of South Carolina. Given under our Hands & Seal this 25th day of October 1726.

Signed,

Entered 6th Dec<sup>r</sup> 1726
by Ri. Shelton, Sec<sup>ty</sup>

Cognit p̄r infra noiat
Henricum Bertie
6 die Februarii
1726 in Cur'
Sign'd
Alex. Denton.

CARTERET P.
BEAUFORT.
CRAVEN.
JA: BERTIE.
HEN: BERTIE.
JOHN TYRRELL.
J. COLLETON.

(L. S.)

( 2 )

[ENDORSEMENT.]—L<sup>r</sup> from M<sup>r</sup> Tho: Lowndes to y<sup>e</sup> Sec<sup>ty</sup> dated y<sup>e</sup> 16th of Feb<sup>ry</sup> 1728/9 relating to his Services in promoting the Purchase of Carolina by the Crown from the L<sup>ds</sup> Proprietors.

Rec<sup>d</sup> 16 Feb<sup>ry</sup> 1728/9
Read July 16, 1729

Sir,

Hearing that the Lords Commissioners for Trade are teazed by Pretenders to Merit in bringing about the purchase of Carolina. I take the liberty to transmit to you a Copy of the Reasons which last year I drew and which were presented to and approved of by the Speaker of the House of Commons and Sixteen other Members, when the Demand was made for the Purchase Money in Parliament.

The Proposal of attacking Fort Augustino and obstructing from Port Royal in South Carolina the Spanish Navigation was first made by me to a Person of great figure in the Administration in May next will be three years and was then liked. What service I have since done in obviating any difficulty that might happen, and in removing obstructions that arose whilst the Bargain for Carolina was negociating a noble Lord of your Board (whose Justice and Honour are equal to his Title) will I doubt not readily vouch for me. And I have ample Testimony of the Pains I have since taken to keep Matters between the Crown and the Proprietors from being inflamed.

Colonel Lilly was too candid a Gentleman not to own publickly the assistance I gave him in drawing his Map of Carolina; I having the most Authentic manuscript Map of that Country and of Port Royal in particular. For as for poor Governour Rogers, his is only an unnatural Fiction, for there can be no such place as he represents Port Royal to be till the nature of water is altered and the Globe new moulded.

I likewise enclose a Copy of a Letter from Governour Craven which I doubt not will give the Lords of Trade satisfaction, he being a Gent of known honour, and I had a Liberty to do with it as I judged proper.

I beg leave to observe to you that it is my humble Opinion that the

Spaniards make their clamorous Mem^m about the little Fort upon Allatamaha River, to conceal their Intentions of getting from us by Treaty the Territory we have upon the Gulf of Mexico. For the Bay of Apalachia is most certainly ours. And it is highly probable there is a good Harbour, either at the Entrance of the River de Guisare, or the River Flint. And the country is esteemed very fertile and the Indians that did inhabit it are either chased away or killed. Of what use it may be to the Spanish nation to have such a Concession or of what prejudice to us to grant it, the Lords Commissioners for Trade are the best judges. I am Sir

16 Feb. 172$\frac{8}{9}$.  Your Most obedient and most humble Servant

P. S.  THO: LOWNDES.

There is I hear a great disposition in the richer Palatins and Germans about Leige to go to South Carolina; So a good Revenue may be made immediately to the King by Quitt Rent.

[*Enclosure.*]

[ENDORSEMENT.]—Copy of a L^r from M^r Craven formerly Governor of Carolina to M^r Tho. Lowndes dated y^e 4^th of May 1726, in relation to the harbour of Port Royal in South Carolina & Timber & other Products at that Place.

Rec^d from M^r Lowndes with his Letter a Copy 16. Feb^y 1728–9.
Rec^d 16 Feb^y 1728–9.
Read

Sir,
Having received yours dated April 16^th 1726 in relation to Port Royal in South Carolina I can only give this Account.

There is water enough for any Ships to come over the Barr. I had it sounded when I was Governour, but through the Carelessness of my Servant my Papers are lost.

It is my Opinion it may be very easily fortified at a small expense to secure the Trade from any Damage from Enemys.

As to the Timber near Port Royal it is as good as in any part of the Continent.

There are several Sorts of Oak for Building, Pine for Masts of Ships and the Land very fertile and proper for Flax and Hemp or any other Grain or Product and great plenty of good Cattle & Fish.

I am &c.  May 4^th 1726.
CHA: CRAVEN.

Mem^d. Lowndes had a Liberty to use M^r Craven's Letter as he should think proper.

( 3 )

[ENDORSEMENT.]—Letter from M^r Tho: Lowndes to the Sec^y dated 23^rd Dec^r 1729, signifying the names of the Patent Officers in South Carolina.

Rec^d 24^th Dec^r 1729 }
Read March 13^th 172$\frac{9}{30}$ }

Sir,
The Officers of Carolina that are within the intention of the saving Clause of the Act for Purchasing Carolina are Edward Bertie Esq. Secre-

tary and Register for Two Lives, myself for Two Lives, Provost Marshall Clerk of the Peace and Crown.

M[r] Robert Wright, was appointed Chief Justice for Life But he, having never been possessed of his Patent and some of the Ministers urging of what ill consequence it might be to have that Officer for Life, Twas agreed that notwithstanding the saving Clause that Patent should be delivered up to the Lord Commis[rs] for Trade to be cancelled and that it should be an Article in the Governour's Instructions to appoint Mr. Wright his Majesties Chief Justice of South Carolina during his Majesties Pleasure only. I know M[r] Wright's Patent is ready to be delivered to the Lords of Trade any day. I am, Sir, your most obedient and most
humble servant
23 Dec[r] 1729.        Tho: Lowndes.

( 4 )

[Endorsement.]—South Carolina. Letter from M[r] Tho[s]: Lowndes of y[e] 24[th] of March 1730 relating to a Clause in an Act of South Carolina for y[e] better settling of y[e] Courts of Justice in that Province.

Rec[d]
Read } March 26. 1731.

Sir,

'Tis with the greatest Confusion, that I beg pardon of the Lords Commissioners for Trade, for giving their Lordships this farther Trouble, which really is occasioned by an Innocent Mistake, and I intreat you, at a proper time to move their Lordships to give Directions (in relation to the Clause requiring Security of the Provost Marshall) agreeable to their Intentions which this day they were so good as to express. For I never had an opportunity to peruse the act of assembly till to-day, after I was called for in, and only hearing it read over before at M[r] Counsellour Fanes Chamber, I took it that the Deputy Provost Marshall was required to give the Security, and accordingly had made provision for it, but their Lordships Candour and Goodness make me sensible of my Misapprehension.

The Complaint of the Merchants and the Point in Issue before M[r] Fane was whether the summons should be restored or the Capias continued, not but that Gent asked if there was any other objection to any part else of the Act, and the Merchants answered " Nothing material."

In all the Plantations that are Royal Governm[ts] these are, (as I am informed) standing Laws, that no Deputy shall be admitted to execute his Office till he has given such security as is agreeable to the Nature of his Office and as is specified in such laws; and the Notion of that and my only hearing the Act very hastily run over was what lead me into the Error and is the Cause of this Application. I am with the greatest respect
Sir
Your most obed[t]
and most humble
Servant
24 March
1730
Tho: Lowndes.

To Allured Popple Esq
Secretary to the Lords Commissioners
for Trade and Plantations.

( 5 )

Plantations General. Patents. Vol. 52. Page 91.

Tho: Lowndes Provost
Marshall in South
Carolina
1730

GEORGE R.

Our Will and Pleasure is that you prepare a bill for our Royal Signature to pass our Great Seal of Great Britain containing our Grant unto our Trusty and Wellbeloved *Thomas Lowndes Esq$^r$* & his Assigns of the Offices or Places of Provost Marshall Clerk of the Peace and Clerk of the Crown of and in our Province of South Carolina in America during the natural lives of the said Thomas Lowndes and Hugh Watson of the Middle Temple Gent: He the said Thomas Lowndes having surrendered unto Us a grant of the said Offices for the lives of him and the said Hugh Watson under the seal of the late Lords Proprietors: To have, hold and enjoy the said offices unto him the said Thomas Lowndes and his assigns for and during his own Life and the Life of the said Hugh Watson and the Survivor of them to be executed by him the said Thomas Lowndes or his assigns or their sufficient Deputy or Deputies; together with all their Salaries, Fees. Perquisites, Profits, Advantages and Privileges whatsoever to the said Offices belonging, in a full and ample manner to all Intents and Purposes as any Person or Persons have heretofore held and enjoy'd or of Right ought to have held and enjoy'd the same and you are to insert in the said Bill all such clauses as are usual, and as you shall judge a Requisite in this Behalf. And for so doing this shall be your Warrant.

Given at our Court at St. James's the Thirtieth day of November 1730 in the Fourth year of our Reign.

By His Majesty's Command
HOLLES NEWCASTLE.

To our Attorney }
or Sollicitor General }

( 6 )

[ENDORSEMENT.]—L$^r$ from M$^r$. T. Lowndes inclosing the Extract of a L$^r$ to him from M$^r$ Wright, Chief Justice of South Carolina dated y$^e$ 6$^{th}$ of August 1731 about repealing y$^e$ Act passed there for bringing Debtors into Court by Capias and thereby reviving y$^e$ Act for a Sumons in lieu thereof.

Recd. Oct. 26; }
Read Nov. 16; } 1731.

Sir,

I take the liberty to inclose two Paragraphs of M$^r$ Wright's Letter to me dated 6$^{th}$ August 1731 from South Carolina, where you know he is his Majesties Chief Justice; You'll please to communicate the same to the Lords Commissioners for Trade and Plantations. And I beg you'll observe to their Lordships that by Act of Assembly a Sallary is settled on the Chief Justice, which with the old Sallary out of the Quitt Rents will make £200 per An$^m$. And I suppose long before this they have passed the Jury-Bill, because they had it under consideration in the middle of last April; so that the Capias Act so prejudicial to Trade and so obstructive to Common Justice may (if their Lordships think proper) be repealed without any sort of Inconveniency in any other respect.

I am
Sir

26 October 1731

Your most obed<sup>t</sup> and
Most humble Servant
THOS: LOWNDES.

Secret<sup>y</sup> to the Board of Trade

( 7 )

[ENDORSEMENT.]—Letter from Mr. Tho: Lowndes in relation to the Capias and Summons Process in South Carolina.

My Lords

In order to set the Capias and Summons Process in South Carolina in a clear light, I beg leave humbly to observe to your Lord<sup>ps</sup> that in all parts of America (Islands as well as others) the Capias was the original Process. But in such places as the Climate or Product required many Negroes, whenever there came to be a great disproportion of Slaves to White People, then the summons was found necessary to be introduced, to aid the Capias. For near the first forty years in South Carolina the Process was by Capias only, nor would any other be now required was the Province in the same Condition it was then. But about the year 1713 when the number of Negroes was increased they instituted the Summons Act (I believe) for two Years at first and afterwards it was made Indeffinite. In the year 1720 it being thought too severe as to the Double milage and Double Process, it was remedied by an Act of Assembly which was also Indeffinite. About the year 1726 after the Merchants had given the Planters very large Credit, the Planters in a very tumultuous manner got (by Act of Assembly) the Summons superseded, and the Capias introduced again. And here I beg leave to hint of what ill consequence it may be, to have an Act which immediately concerns the Property of the British Merchants repealed, only by some loose general Words without so much as reciting the Act, which is the Case here in point before your Lordships.

I entirely agree with M<sup>r</sup> Johnson as to the Abuses committed by the Provost Marshalls in South Carolina. And the case was thus. The late Lords Proprietors, for their Governour's Emolument always permitted them to nominate the Provost Marshall, who was accountable to the Governours for half Profits and sometimes more, and for this Reason the Marshall was generally protected in all his unjustifiable Practices. But now the Acting Provost Marshall is to give Security (as is highly reasonable) to answer for all mal-Practices; That Officer will be obliged to the faithfull Execution of his Office in South Carolina as well as in Jamaica and other parts of America. For had the Practices of the Provost Marshall been not to be remedied after thirteen years tryal of the Summons Act, one would reasonably have expected to have found some mention at least of such ill behaviour in the Act of 1726 which repeals the Summons. And M<sup>r</sup> Johnson takes no notice of the hazard of his Life that the Marshall now runs in serving the Capias out of Charles Town, the frequent Rescues from the Officer, how the Negroes are let loose upon him, and he frequently whiped or drawn through a Ditch, and all Complaints upon this head are to no purpose; for legal Proof cannot be made that it was by their Master's order, tho' every one knows it could not be done without it. And these Irregularities which cannot otherwise be prevented were the Cause of the Summons both in South Carolina, Jamaica, Barbados and other places where the Negroes are numerous.

Your Lordships I am sure will observe the Proviso in the Act of the year 1720 for the Amendm[t] of the law whereby thirty days is allowed before Execution on Judgm[t] shall be granted, if the Party be brought into Court by Summons, in which time it is hardly possible but he must be apprized of what is going on against him, unless he be an Indian Trader, for whom I some time ago took the Liberty to propose a Remedy. And if the Party be summoned upon an account not to be maintained he has ample Redress against his Adversary by Law.

I most humbly offer to your Lordships Consideration, his Majesties Letters Patent to me for the Office of Provost Marshall, the benefit of which I am entirely deprived of by the present Capias Act, and (not of Modesty) I kept from complaining till your Lordships had heard from M[r] Johnson upon that head, but now I must desire your Lordships to hear and redress my Complaint.

The last part of M[r] Johnson's Letter is very fallacious. For of what use can it be to the Merchants that they may try the causes out of the Precinct Courts where they may have fair Juries, unless they can bring their Debtors (the Planters) into Court, which five miles out of Charles Town they cannot do unless the Summons be restored?

The real truth, my Lords, is that the greatest part of the Planters being indebted to the Merchants, M[r] Johnson is afraid of doing anything that may disoblige the Planters, especially at this Juncture, his Appointment being by the Country only granted for One Year. I humbly conjure your Lordships to hear the Act for the Amendment of the Law read and then your Lordships will be convinced that nothing is desired but what is absolutely necessary for the obtaining Common Justice. I am with the greatest respect

My Lords
Your Lordships
Most obedient and
Most humble Servant
THOS: LOWNDES.

14 Dec[r] 1831

P. S. If the Objection that the Act for the Amendem[t] of the Law, was passed by Gov[r] More be allowed, several of the best Acts will be void and great confusion ensue in the Province.

( 8 )

[ENDORSEMENT.]—Mem[l] from M[r] Lowndes against *an Act* of South Carolina *declaring all Process to be voyd that was not personally served upon the Party by the Provost Marshall or his Deputy;* and ab[t] the Want of Provision for Indigent Criminals.

To the Right Honourable the Lords Commissioners for Trade and Plantations.

The humble Memorial of Thomas Lowndes Sheweth

That about two or three years ago there passed in South Carolina an Act declaring all Process to be void, that was not personally served upon the Party, by the Provost Marshall or his Deputy which act makes the Execution of Common justice not only difficult but impracticable; and is very prejudicial to the Commerce of Great Britain. For no Merchant will now furnish any Commoditys to a Planter that lives at any distance from Charles Town because he cannot be compelled to be just and the Planter is thereby forced to go upon such Manufactures as interfere with those of Great Britain.

That this Evil will be of very bad consequence if not speedily redressed either by re-authorizing the Summons Act, or by some other Method as your Lordships shall think proper.

Your Memorialist also begs leave to observe That there wants in South Carolina a Suitable Publick Provision for indigent Criminals, it being equally inhuman that those poor Wretches should perish through want of common sustenance, as it is unreasonable that the Provost Marshall or his Deputy should subsist them at his own proper Charge.

All which is most humbly submitted to your Lordships great Judgement and wisdome.   THOS: LOWNDES.

( 9 )

[ENDORSEMENT.]—Letter from Colonel Johnson dated Charles Town 28th September 1732 to Allured Popple Esq. complaining of Mr Thos: Lowndes having ill-treated him in relation to the Summons Law and Deputy Marshals Place in South Carolina.

Recd Decr 22nd 1732
Read Aug 27th 1735.

[*Extract.*]

"I am in great pain for fear I should lye under your Lordships censure, having had a Copy of Mr Lowndes Memorial sent me, which he told Mr Fury he designed to prefer against me, setting forth that I did not obey your Lordships orders in recommending to the Assembly the repealing of the Capias Act, that I did is certain, and does appear by a Message of the 18th of August 1731, which notorious falsity I hope will give him little credit with your Lordships for the future; he has also asserted that I have made the Marshalls place a perquisite of my Government, which is likewise false, I found Mr Bampfield Marshal I continued him at his own request as is notorious to all the Province, I appointed a person of his recommending, he telling me he desired to be dismist, because his affairs required his going to England, and about six months after he told me he had altered his mind and desired to be restored, which I granted him, and he was lately unfortunately drowned. I defy Lowndes to prove I had any profit by this; but did it only to serve a man I thought was worthy of the place, and one Mr Popple had a friendship for. Mr Lowndes has sent no exemplification of his Patent nor appointed any deputy, in the mean time the office must be supplied, so how I have wronged him above £200 as he has told my friends, I can't find out, nor he neither I am sure, 'tis very hard to have my actions so misrepresented, by one that has cunningly made this Province his property by the late Lords Proprietors neglect to the amount of £4000 or £5000 Stg: nobody knows for what other merit than a consumate assurance, pretending to know everything, betraying everybody and altering his opinion as often as he finds it for his Interest; I find his Malice to me proceeds from my giving your Lord$^{ps}$ my opinion that the Assembly will hardly ever be brought to inforce the Summons Law and I found it so when I sent to them about it; That Law was disannuled before my time, I have no Interest one way or other in it; 'tis my Duty to give your Lordships my opinion of things, I obeyed your Orders and recommended the repeal of it, but to no purpose; it now lyes with your Lordships to report as you please about it, but am sure your Lord$^{ps}$ wont think a Legislature of a Province is to pass Laws they disapprove of, purely to serve M$^r$ Lowndes Interest, or because as he sets forth his Interest is hurt; that is he won't have so good an opportunity of getting £1500 St$^g$: which is his price for the Marshals place, not intrinsically worth £700 altho' the Capias Law was repealed; the hopes of which keeps him from letting it, for fear of depreciating the sale of it; for he is sensible that nobody that knows the value of it will give him above 50 or £60 a year for it."

### Copy of M$^r$ Lowndes Petition or Memorial.

"That your Pet$^r$ finding a Clause in an Act passed in South Carolina 1726 contrary to a Maxim of the Common Law of England and the Universal Practice of every Colony in America, applyed to the Lords Comm$^{rs}$ for Trade and Plantations to have the same remedyed and their Lordp$^s$ wrote to Governor Johnson about it, an Extract of which Letter is hereunto annexed. But your Petitioner has not been as yet redressed nor likely to be, for tho' the Assembly was sitting at the time M$^r$ Johnson received the Letter from the Lords of Trade and continued to do business for more than two months afterwards yet that Gentleman did not communicate to the Assembly the Order he had received but has made your Petitioner's Office a Perquisite of his Government and appointed a Creature of his own to execute the place who renders your Petitioner no account whatsoever."

( 10 )

[ENDORSEMENT.]—Order of a Committee of Council dated 27 April 1733 referring the Petition of M$^r$ Thorpe for the confirmation of a grant of 9000 Acres of Land in South Carolina.

Rec$^d$ 4: } May 1733.
Read 8: }

To the King's most Excellent Majesty
The humble Petition of Robert Thorpe
Sheweth
That the late Lords Proprietors of Carolina by Grant under their Common Seal bearing date the 25$^{th}$ day of October 1726 Did give and convey unto Isaac Lowndes his heirs and Assignes one Barrony or Tract of Land to contain 12000 Acres Subject to one penny Sterling quit rent which Grant did likewise authorize and require the Surveyor General of the Province of South Carolina immediately within 20 days after Notice given him thereof to allott and Sett out the said Tract or Barrony of Land in any Place within the said Province of South Carolina.

That the said Isaac Lowndes by deed bearing date the 26$^{th}$ day of August

1729 for himself, his heirs and Assigns Did declare and agree that his name was made use of in the said Grant from the Lords Proprietors only as Trustee to and for the use and behoof of Thomas Lowndes of the City of Westminster Gentleman his heirs and Assigns and to and for no other Purpose whatsoever.

That the said Isaac Lowndes and Thos: Lowndes in Consideration of the sum of £450 Lawfull money of Great Brittain to the said Tho$^s$ Lowndes in hand paid by your Petitioner and also in Consideration of 5 Shillings of Like Lawfull money to the said Isaac Lowndes well and truly paid by your Petitioner Did by deeds Indented bearing Date the 10$^{th}$ Day of Sep$^r$ 1731, Grant, Bargain, sell and Confirm unto your Petitioner his Heirs and Assigns a Tract of Land to Contain 9000 Acres English Measure being part of the said Barrony so granted as aforesaid to Isaac Lowndes in trust for the said Thomas Lownds.

That your Petitioner having thus purchased the aforesaid tract of 9000 Acres Did apply to James St John Esq$^r$ your Majestys Surveyor General of the Province of South Carolina to allott and sett out the said Barrony so granted as Aforesaid who readily performed the same that your Petitioner did thereupon take possession of his part thereof.

That your Petitioner nevertheless finding Doubts arise concerning the Legallity of such Survey it being made without a Warrant had from your Majestys Gov$^t$ empowering the Surveyor General so to doe, And finding also the said Governor Deny granting Warrants to survey Lands claimed under Patents or Grants from the Late Lords Proprietors without knowing your Majestys Pleasure concerning such Grants notwithstanding that in an act passed in the 2 year of your Majestys reign entitled an Act for establishing an Agreement with seven of the Lords Proprietors of Carolina for the Surrender of their Title and Interest in that Province to his Majesty. There is an Exception in these words Except all such Tracts of Land, Tenements and Hereditaments as have been at any time before the first Day of January 1727 granted and conveyed or comprized in any Grants Deeds, Instruments or Conveyances under the Common Seal of the said Lords Proprietors either in England or in the province aforesaid.

He therefore most humbly prays your Majesty

That as he is Seized of the said Tract of Land by a Title derived from the Late Lords Proprietors long before the time of the Surrender of their Respective Interest to your Majesty and that for the Valuable Consideration of £450 lawfull money of Great Brittain Your Majesty to prevent his being molested in the quiet possession of the same would be graciously pleased to direct your Governor of the said Province that your Petitioner may not any wise be molested in his possession of the said Lands conveyed to him as aforesaid before the Surrender to your Majesty and also expressly excepted by the aforesaid Act of Parliament out of the said Surrender.

And your Petitioner as in duty Bound shall ever pray

ROBERT THORPE.

( 11 )

[ENDORSEMENT.]—Letter from M$^r$ Tho: Lowndes in relation to M$^r$ Thorpe's Grant of Land in South Carolina.

Recd May 21$^{st}$ } 1733
Read D$^o$ 22:

My Lords

In obedience to your Lordships' commands of the 11th Instant, directing me to lay a State of a Transaction relating to 9000 Acres of Land, sold by me to Mr Thorpe, I most humbly beg leave to acquaint your Lordships that about eighteen months ago I sold to that Gentleman and Mr De la Fontaine One Barony in South Carolina to contain Twelve Thousand Acres of Land Vizt 9000 to Mr Thorpe and Three to Mr De la Fontaine for which they paid me the money contracted for. The words in the conveyances were these *Land not yet admeasured taken up or run out in the province of South Carolina*. A little after the writings were perfected, Mr Thorpe went to South Carolina and there finding that an Agent for me had by my direction (many months before my Agreement with him) run out a Barony upon Port Royal River, Mr Thorpe liking the situation applied to him, and falsely aver'd that the Barony so run out, was the Identical Barony he and Mr De la Fontaine had bought of me. By which means (and a present as I am informed) he prevailed upon my agent not to return into the Surveyor's Office the Field Survey he had made; Mr Thorpe also got Mr St John his Majesties Surveyour General to survey the same Tract for him, and to return and certify the Plan. As soon as I was informed of this proceeding, I wrote to Mr De la Fontaine about it, who I always found ready to make me any reasonable Satisfaction, so far as he was concerned, and only deferred it, till Mr Thorpe returned. Upon his arrival I expostulated civilly with him, and let him know the injury he had done me, I having a grant for 12000 Acres which must now be taken up in a more remote part of the Country. I found him not inclined to do me any sort of justice, but instead of that affirmed many absurd untruths. Upon the coming over lately of some Persons of Credit from South Carolina Mr Thorpe believing that I should by them disprove what he had advanced made application to the Lords of his Majtys Privy Council to procure an Order, under the Sanction of which he hop'd (as I humbly presume) to keep in possession of the Land he had unfairly entred upon and baffle any Remedy at law I might endeavor to get.

Tho' this is the true State of the Law yet I proposed for Peace Sake to leave the matter in Dispute to Arbitration, as the enclosed copy of an extract of my Letter to Mr De la Fontaine will shew your Lordships.

If your Lordps write to Mr De la Fontaine to lay before your Lordps a Copy of such part of Mr Thorpe's first Letter from Carolina as relates to the running out of the Barony (which I am sure he is too fair a man to refuse doing, he having formerly communicated it to me) your Lordps will clearly see how uncandidly Mr. Thorpe has dealt with me. I am very much concerned that Mr Thorpe's conduct should occasion my giving your Lordps this Trouble. I am with the greatest respect
   My Lords
    Your Lordships
     Most obedient and
      Most humble Servant

19 May 1733             THOS: LOWNDES.

[*Minute, probably by the Secretary.*]

Several Particulars wherein Messrs Thorpe's and De la Fontaines Grant purchased from Thomas Lowndes differ from other Grants of Land made by the late Lords Proprietors. There was no non-user in any respect incurred upon this Grant.

There is a Warrant in the Body of those Grants that were Lowndes's to the Survey[r] Gen[l] to run out the Land by a time therein limitted, so that Thorpe had no occasion to apply to the Governour for his Warrant.

Lowndes's Grants were likewise given in by name in writing to the Lords of his Majesties most honourable Privy Council at the time of the Treaty for purchasing Carolina, that they might most evidently be known not to be within the Intention of the Crowns Purchase. The Grant purchased by Thorpe is more advantagious than the Reciprocal Grants of the late Lords Propr[ts] to themselves, except in respect of the Descent of Election which as Lowndes has been informed is peculiar to such Reciprocal Grants.

The words in Thorpe's Grant amount to a Warranty, which for me was not used in the Common Grants and the Crown with respect to the Purchase of Carolina (tis humbly presumed) stands in the Place of the late Lords Proprietors.

The condition upon Non-performance of which Lowndes's Grant sold to Thorpe was to be void was punctually observed viz[t] It was enrolled in the Court of Common Pleas within the time limited by the Grant, as the Inrollment makes appear.

N. B. Lowndes's Grant sold to Thorpe is entered in the Plantation Office and so is the Purchase Deed.

( 12 )

[ENDORSEMENT.]—Letter from Mr. Thos: Lowndes in relation to the Grants of land in South Carolina.

Chiswick 4[th] June 1733.

Sir,

Being requested (as you know) by one of the Lords Commissioners for Trade, to set in a fuller light (than in my last) the Difference that there is between the Common Grants for Land in Carolina to Private Grantees, and the Grants made by the Lords Prop[rs] to themselves, I beg leave to observe that Carolina having never made but very inconsiderable (if any) Profit by the Quit Rents (after paying the Expence of Govern[mt]) it was usual for the Lords Proprie[ts] from time to time to make reciprocal Grants to themselves at a Pepper-Corn Rent which were sold or disposed of to be run out at the pleasure of the Purchaser or other lawfull owner. These Grants tho' not run out or taken up in the life-time of the Grantee were descendable to the Purchaser or owner or their Representatives.

The Common Grants to Private Grantees, tho' they were to Heirs of Executors Adm[rs] and assigns were never deemed to convey any Property unless taken up or run out in the life time of the Grantee and were no more than Warrants of Election which were wholly extinguished by the Death of the Grantee. There was many times equitable Circumstances which induced the Proprietors not to take Advantage of such Extinguishm[t]. As the Eminent Services of the Grantee, a Suddain Indian War, being taken Prisoner in going over to take Possession and dying in the Ennemies hands and many other Accidents. The Lord Carteret as I have been informed some short time ago, sold to several Considerable Merchants and others his Baronys, it would Sure be very unreasonable that in case Lord Carteret the Grantee should dye before the laying out their Baronys that the Purchasers should lose their right to run them out. This is very likely the case of some others who claim under Reciprocal Grants. But the Common Grantees were not Purchasers, only paid a Rent after the Land was run out.

The legal Reason for this Distinction (as I have been told) and for which I referr myself to M$^r$ Vane arose from this. The Lords Proprietors were seized in fee as Tenants in Common and each of them had full Possession of One undivided Eighth Part and such Reciprocal Grants were only small separate parts of what before was contained in such Undivided Shares or Parts. But the Common Grantees (unless they run out their Lands) had no Seizin and therefore their Lands could not descend.

If any doubt should remain with that learned Gent I believe I can produce to him an Instance from the Legislature which will put the Right of such as claim under Reciprocal Grants to Proprietors beyond all possibility of Dispute.

So that I beg leave to add that the most evident and essential Difference between the Grants made to Me and the Common Grants is, that mine were not void being run out in the life time of the Grantee, all Grants being void if not run out before the Death of the Grantees except such as derive their Right of Claim from any Reciprocal Grant to the late Lords Proprietors. Did I not know the Lords of Trade to be persons of great Honour I should not express myself with such Frankness. For I have a Barony undisposed of, and I am in a declining way tho' in Equity I may be justly deemed a Purchaser.

I am Sir
Your most obedient and
Most humble Servant
THO: LOWNDES.

P. S. As to the No. of Barony's not disposed of by the Proprietors and included in the Crowns Purchase if I remember right they are particularly specified in the Act of Parliament.

( 13 )

ENDORSEMENT.—L$^r$ from M$^r$ Tho: Lowndes to Sir Orlando Bridgeman relating to a Misconstruction of Col: Johnson's Instruction for granting of Land.

Recd. 12: } June 1733.
Read 22: }

JUNE 12$^{th}$ 1733.

Sir,
I take the Liberty to acquaint your Honour and the rest of the Lords Comm$^{rs}$ for Trade and Plantations that there is a most scandalous, unreasonable Interpretation put upon an Article in the Governour of South Carolina's Instructions, and the Province will be involved in great Difficultys if a Remedy be not speedily applyed. The abuse is committed under the name of Family Warrants. Many hundred Thousand Acres of the Choisest Land, upon the best Rivers are run out under the pretence of complying with an Order which was wisely intended for the Good of the Province and which without abandoning all common understanding, and

Common Honesty could never have been wrested as it has been. It is the latter Part of the 42 Article, that they force to give a Sanction to their Proceedings. I believe the Lords of Trade have not yet been informed of this unprecedented Transaction.

I also beg leave to observe to you and the rest of their Lordships that there is (I humbly conceive) a thing in my power to lay before your Board, and which if not timely discovered and prevented will occasion a great deal of trouble to the Lords of Trade, and be of very ill consequence to the Publick, and their Lordships Correspondents (I believe) can't inform them of this Particular till it is too late. I will undertake candidly to shew their Lordships the whole Affair. But then I hope I may be allowed to depend upon having (as a reward for the Service) their Lordships Favour and Protection in any Application I shall hereafter make to them, where I have Justice, Equity or Reason on my Side.

Your Honour can't have forgot that when the Lords of Trade through misrepresentations to them had settled the Quitt Rent in South Carolina at 2 shill p Hundred Acres Proclamation Money, I gave you some Information (to be depended on) that the Land would bear a much higher Rent, upon which their Lordships altered their Resolution and settled the Quitt Rent as it now stands.

You'll please to indulge me by letting M$^r$ Docminique know that he misunderstood what I said at your Board the other day, when (amongst other things) I asked him "whether I had expressed myself clearly enough." For that Question had no reference to the Affair which M$^r$ Thorpe gave their Lordships the trouble of (and where in he now wants to equivocate and explain) but to a Letter relating to Patents which M$^r$ Docminique desired me a few days before to write to the Board; and designing next week to go to France, I thought it but a decent peice of Respect to ask if that Letter wanted Explanation. Your Goodness I hope will pardon this tedious Letter, and allow me the Honour of subscribing myself with the greatest Respect
       Sir,
         Your most obedient and
          Most humble Servant
            Tho: Lowndes.

P. S. I have an utter aversion to the giving Gentlemen of Rank any trouble and if their Lordships referr me to M$^r$ Wheelock or M$^r$ Burnish to explain my self They will have Patience with my weak state of Health, and I know M$^r$ Sec$^{ty}$ Popple has such a vast Load of Business that he can't allow me time to be understood.

Sir Orlando Bridgeman One of the Lords of Trade.

( 14 )

Endorsement.]—Letter from Tho: Lowndes Dated the 2$^{nd}$ June 1733.

Recd ) 
Read ) June 22$^{nd}$ 1733

My Lords,

The Province of Georgia is in imminent danger of being ruined, at least the Settlement will be vastly discouraged, and the intent of the Publick frustrated, and your Lordp$^s$ must have almost endless applications if what I have to propose be not taken immediately under consideration.

I intend to set out for France on Wednesday next, the constant acute Pain I am in renders me unfit for the Honour of having a long Audience at your Lordp$^s$ Board: if the Terms proposed in my last (which I hope are not reckoned immodest) are granted me I will honestly communicate in writing what this matter (which your Lordp$^s$ will find to be of great importance) is.

I am with the greatest respect

My Lords

Your Lordships

Most obedient and

Most humble Servant

22 June 1733.  THO: LOWNDES.

( 15 )

[ENDORSEMENT.]—L$^r$ from Tho: Lowndes dated 25$^{th}$ June 1733 relating to the manner of granting Lands in South Carolina.

Rec$^d$ June 26$^{th}$ }
Read July 4$^{th}$ } 1733

My Lords,

In consequence of a Letter from my self of the 12$^{th}$ Instant to Sir Orlando Bridgeman, One of your Lordship's Board, and also of One other like Letter to your Board of 22 Do. I humbly beg leave to observe to your Lordships that the late Lords Proprietors of Carolina did in June 1717 grant to Sir Robert Montgomery (in trust for another Person) all the Tract of Land between the Rivers Alatamaha and Savannah, with all Islands &c. which grant, tho' really void, is now revived and stands fully confirmed and established by 15$^{th}$ Page of the Printed Copy of an Act passed in South Carolina 1730 entituled an Act for Remission of Arrears of Quitt Rent &c.

The Territory mentioned in Montgomery's Grant is now by his Majestys Letters Patents created into the Province of Georgia.

I am by good Hands informed that the person who pretends to claim under this Grant, intends in a short time to take Possession of it. And if once Possession is got, which in all probability may be done, before the Act is repealed (a Person being now arrived from Carolina to support it, and the Agent praying to shew Cause before the Lords of the Council for its Confirmation) the Claimant must certainly have in view the maintaining his Title by a Subscription, in the year 1720, of a large sum of money made by many Persons of the best Rank and Quality. Great part of which money was said to be expended in buying Arms, Cloaths, Tools, Utensils &c. for settling and cultivating some Islands or part of the Territory mentioned in the above named Grant which Territory or Islands are part of Georgia.

Your Lordships in your Report for repealing this Bill having not objected to the Confirmation of Montgomery's Grant is construed as a tacit acknowledgment of its validity.

In the year 1725 there was a Treaty set on Foot betwixt the late Lords Proprietors and the Persons claiming under the Grant to Sir Robert Montgomery, from which (if once Possession is got) many Arguments for pretended Equity may be drawn. The Papers relating to that Treaty are my Property, and in my Possession and ready to be produced.

The Grant from the late Lords Prop$^{ts}$ is very loosely and improperly worded and affords many advantages to the views the Persons claiming under it may have, if (as the Act of Carolina now stands) the Grant be entred upon.

The various involved and complicated Transactions that have been carried on either really or pretendedly under this Grant to Montgomery may I humbly presume (if care is not taken) occasion your Lordships innumerable applications.

I hope I have made out, what I undertook, and it would be impious in me to doubt the performance of what I was promised on 22$^{nd}$ Instant in the name of your Lordp$^s$ Board, and which I humbly insisted on in my letter of 12$^{th}$ Ins$^t$ as a Reward for this Service viz$^t$ Your Lords$^{ps}$ Favour and Protection in any Application I shall hereafter make to your Lordp$^s$ where I have Justice, Equity or Reason on my side; and I hope not to live to put any Disingenuous Interpretation upon these Words. And I beg your Lordp$^s$ will please to order a Proper Minute upon this Occasion.

The Earl of Westmorland to whose Goodness I have great Obligations, will now see I have done what I took the Liberty to inform his Lord$^p$ I could do in my letter to his Lord$^p$ of 4$^{th}$ May 1732 And I delayed giving your Lordp$^s$ this Information till I saw the Kings Officers who wrote over against this Act to miss the Point; and that the Intent of the Publick as to the Settlement of Georgia was just going to be frustrated.

When the Limits in North America betwixt Great Britain and Spain are to be adjusted, I have something (I presume) of consequence to lay before your Lordp$^s$ Board. I am

       My Lords
25$^{th}$ June 1733.   Your Lordships most obedient
        and most humble Servant
          THO: LOWNDES.

P. S. The Grant to Montgomery is entred at large in one of the late Lords Prop$^{rs}$ Books which (I believe) was delivered in to the Plantation Office upon the Crowns Purchase and there is in another of their Books a Mem$^d$ of this Grant given in by the late Prop$^{rs}$ to the Lords of the Council at the time of the said Purchase which for your Lordp$^s$ Perusal M$^r$ Wheelock permitted me to look out. Azilia and the Golden Islands are all in the same Grant to Montgomery.

( 16 )

[ENDORSEMENT.]—Letter of Mr. Tho: Lowndes in relation to Col. Horsey's Grant of Land in South Corolina.

My Lords,
  Being at present a little at ease from two violent Distempers, with which I was tortured when I drew up my late Petition to your Lordships, and reflecting calmly upon every step that was taken in his Majesties Purchase of the Carolina Charter, I do from the Circumstances of things aver,

that Col. Horsey's Warrant for the 48000 Acres of Land could not possibly be signed till Feb$^y$ 172$\frac{7}{y}$ after the Treaty with the Crown was set on Foot. And the late Lords Proprietors who are men of Quality and Persons of great Justice and Honour, will to be sure give your Lordships a satisfactory reason, why Col. Horsey's Warrant was antedated, for that Transaction I was in no wise privy to.

I am with the greatest Respect<br>
My Lords<br>
Your Lordships<br>
Most obedient and<br>
Most humble Servant<br>
THO: LOWNDES.

25 Feb$^y$. 173$\frac{3}{4}$.

Tricks will be plaid with the Propr$^{rs}$ Minute Book if care be not taken.

Lords Com$^{rs}$ for Trade.

NOTE.—Mr. Lowndes had submitted on the 23d of February, three days previous, a lengthy memorial to the Lords Commissioners for Trade, objecting to Horsey's pretensions to a claim of 48,000 acres.

( 17 )

[ENDORSEMENT.]—L$^{tr}$ from M$^r$ Tho: Lowndes of 26 Feb. 173$\frac{3}{4}$ to the Sec$^{ty}$ containing nothing of Office or publick business only general Reflections on the Secretary.

Rec$^d$ Feb 26: } 173$\frac{3}{4}$
Read    28: }

Sir,

In return for a gross incivility you was guilty of some time ago towards me, I intend in a few days to print in the Grub Street Journal some letters of yours to me, *wrote in your private Capacity;* and being a letter in your debt was the reason I wrote my last to you in that style and manner.

But really I must Congratulate the Publick that a Person so engaged in Business as you are have been able to improve the Orthography of our language without putting the State to the Expence of an Academy.

I am Sir<br>Your most humble Serv$^t$<br>THO: LOWNDES.

Feb. 26$^{th}$ 173$\frac{3}{4}$.

( 18 )

[ENDORSEMENT.]—L$^{tr}$ from M$^r$ Tho: Lowndes dated Oct. 22$^{nd}$ 1734 relating to his Grant of Land in South Carolina and to that part of it sold to M$^r$ Rutherford.

Rec$^d$. } Oct$^r$ 22: 1734.
Read }

22$^{nd}$ Oct$^r$ 1734.

My Lords,

I must be allowed the Liberty to observe to your Lord$^{ps}$ that about four years ago I sold a Barony of Land in South Carolina the Grant of which except the Trustees name was just the same with that purchased by M$^r$ Rutherford (which has long lain in your Lord$^{ps}$ Office) and I took bonds payable at a future Day for the Purchase Money. Some time after the Bonds were become due I put them in Suit, and the Security, one M$^r$ Cotton of Cutler's Hall an Attorney of much fame by direction as he said of Wright the Purchaser brought a Bill in the Exchequer at Westm$^r$ Praying that the Bonds might be delivered up cancelled, *for that the Grant for the purchase of which They were given was void for uncertainty there being no Bounds, Metes or Limits described in it.*

I by order of Court set forth the Grant in haec Verba and pleaded the Saving Clause in the Act of Parliament for the Crown's Purchase of Carolina and my answer was not only allowed to be sufficient and good, but after several Hearings before the Lord Chief Baron & the Three other Barons the Purchaser's Bill was dismissed with full Costs; which together with the Purchase Money was levyed upon the Securitys, Goods &c. in Hertfordshire and Middlesex. Your Lordships Solicitor may give you full Information of the whole proceedings, for we fought all the weapons through.

The Records of the Council Office of the 19$^{th}$ March 172$\frac{7}{8}$ will shew (when the Treaty was negociating) that his Majesty bought Carolina with the Incumbrance of my Grant, expressly and by name. And the saving Clause was accordingly drawn by the Grant now before your Board. If after all this my Right is to be questioned, I know not what can be called Property.

M$^r$ Ward and M$^r$ Pigott have drawn all the deeds for the Land I have sold and they aver my Title to be without Exception. *For his Majesty (with all submission I write it) is bound in Law by the Proprietor's Warranty which is peculiar to my Grant alone.* And I was a Purchaser for a Valuable Consideration.

I therefore beg leave humbly to insist on your Lordships performing your Agreement with me as to directing the Surveyor Gen$^l$ to run out the Barony sold to M$^r$ Rutherford agreeable to my memorial. The Surveyor Gen$^l$ is an Officer under your Lordship's Directions by his Instructions.

I most solemnly Conjure your Lordships not to let your Prejudice to my person affect my cause when you sit in Judgement. The complaint I exhibited against your Secretary M$^r$ Popple was well grounded, for I was basely cheated by his mediation and I lost more than Sixty Pounds.

I do with truth assure your Lordships did I not abhorr disserving my native Country I can shew a neighboring nation how to deprive Great Britain of a valuable Branch of Trade without infringing any Treaty, and if your Lordships will signify that you think this a vain Bragg (so that my honour as an Englishman may be fully justifyed) I will immediately and publickly set down in writing how in that particular Our commerce may be prejudiced; and I know my Lords how to be very welcome to a foreign State whose Language, Manners and Customs ('tis well known) I am no stranger to.

      I am my Lords
       Your Lordships
        Most oppressed humble Ser$^t$
         THO: LOWNDES.

( 19 )

[ENDORSEMENT.]—The Provost Marshall's Petition for an allowance out of the Quit Rents for the charge he has been at in building a Provincial Gaol.

Recd } Oct. 31, 1735.
Read }

To the Queen's most Excellent Majesty in Council. The Humble Petition of *George Morley Esq* Provost Marshall of His Majesty's Province of South Carolina in America,

Most humbly Sheweth

That your Peti<sup>r</sup> holds the said Office under an Assignment of his Majesty's Letters Patent bearing date the 11<sup>th</sup> day of February in the Fourth year of his Reign which he has since executed with great care, Diligence and Fidelity.

That your Pet<sup>r</sup> has been at great expence in going over to Carolina to put the said Office into Order and in accomplishing thereof he found very great Difficultys, and there being no salary annexed to the Office nor any Provincial Gaol for the confinement of prisoners your Pet<sup>r</sup> has been obliged at his own loss and charges to hire a house and fit it up in a proper and suitable manner.

That the Profits arising therefrom are very small though the Trust is great.

That the Interest and property of many of His Majesty's Subjects of the said Province depends upon a due execution of the said Office and keeping in safe Custody from time to time the Prisoners Committed to his Charge.

Your Petitioner therefore most humbly prays Your Majesty that you will be graciously pleased to grant him such an allowance out of the Quit Rents of that Province as may enable him to provide for the better Security of the Prisoners and encourage his Diligence in the faithful Execution of his office on which the good government of the Province does so immediately depend.

And your Petitioner as in Duty bound shall ever pray

GEO: MORLEY.
reed from M<sup>r</sup> Furie

( 20 )

At the Court of Kensington 15 July 1736.

Present The Queen's most excellent Majesty and his Majesty's Lieutenant.

Her Majesty was pleased by her Order in Council of the 13<sup>th</sup> of October last to refer to the Consideration of a Committee of the Privy Council the humble Petition of George Morley Esq<sup>r</sup> that they make the necessary Provisions for erecting a Common Goal & keeping the same in repair agreeable to the Practice of other British Colonys.

( 21 )

Extract of a Letter from Colonel Bull dated Charlestown 23<sup>rd</sup> of January 174⅔.

"I further beg leave to acquaint your Lordships the Office of Provost Marshal became vacant by the death of M<sup>r</sup> *Robert Hall* who executed that

Trust under *George Morley Esq*ʳ Assignee of *Thomas Lowndes* the Patentee, and thereupon I did pursuant to his Majestys Instructions fill up that Vacancy by appointing *M*ʳ *William Williamson** to execute the Office of Provost Marshal."

( 22 )

[ENDORSEMENT.]—Letter from Mʳ Lowndes to yᵉ Secretary dated yᵉ 21ˢᵗ of February 1746-7 upon the subject of his Petition lately referred to this Board, relating to a Grant of Land in South Carolina made to him the 25ᵗʰ of October 1726.

Recd Feb'y 21ˢᵗ } 174⁶⁄₇.
Read March 6ᵗʰ

21ˢᵗ Feb'y 1746.

Sir,
    I can indeed do a very considerable service to our American Trade. But why should I break my Brains, when I meet with such Treatment?
    However I beg leave to acquaint the Right Honᵇˡᵉ the Lords Commissioners for Trade and Plantations, that at the time of the Sale of the Carolinas, I was owner of Five Baronys, One in the name of John Beresford, sold to Admiral Anson and Mʳ Wright, One in the name of Isaac Lowndes sold to Messieurs Thorpe and De la Fontaine, One in the name of Charles Edwards run out by Colˡ Bull and myself, One in the name of Wright (mentioned in the Act of Parliament) sold to Mʳ Commissioner Revel and Partners, and One in my own name, the Grant for which is now in your Office.
    If the Prayer of my Petition be granted, this will be the Consequence. His Majesty will thereby extinguish a Grant and future Settlers will by that means pay for Land which otherwise would be covered by my Grant, and the amount of the Quit-Rent so payable will be of the same Value with the present decrease of the Quit-Rents.
    But, permit me to observe, that I have no Common merit with regard to his Majestys Quit-Rents. For they would have been reduced to a Contemptible Pittance, had it not been for the Regulation drawn up by me, which was presented in form to the Lords of Trade, and in a Letter to the Board, previous to giving in the Paper, I insisted that it was to be deemed a publick Service, and as such it was received by the Board.
    Ill-health and ill-fortune together shall not deprive me of the pleasure of reflecting, that by that Performance, his Majesty's troops in North America were kept from suffering very great distress, which could not otherwise have been prevented, as our Law then was and still continues. I had at that time very civil acknowledgments from some of the first persons in the Kingdom, and sure no man did ever ask a more moderate Gratification, than I have petitioned for.

                      I am with great and real respect
                      Sir
                            Your most obedient and
I herewith send a good draft          Most humble Servant
of the island of Ratan which            THO: LOWNDES.
when their Lordˢ have seen,
you'll please to return.

* Williamson, as *late* Provost Marshal, petitioned the Council of South Carolina March 8, 1742-3.

( 23 )

[ENDORSEMENT.]—Letter from James Glen Esq$^r$. Govern$^{nr}$ of South Carolina to the Board dated 27$^{th}$ July 1752.

Rec$^d$ Oct 1752.
Read Nov. 8, 1752.

ABSTRACT.—Acquainting their Lord$^{ps}$ of the death of James Wedderburn Esq$^r$ who enjoyed the Offices of Clerk of the Crown and Peace, and Clerk of the Common Pleas for 20 years & executed them with satisfaction. He held the Office of Clerk of the Common Pleas by Patent under the Great Seal in Consequence of his Majesty's Royal Sign Manual to the governour for that purpose; but enjoyed the Offices of Clerk of the Crown and Peace as Assignee of Thomas Lowndes who had a Grant for the same under the seal of the Lords Propri$^{rs}$ to him, his heirs & Assigns, but having surrendered the same into the hands of his Majesty, His Majesty was graciously pleased to re-grant the said Offices to Thos: Lowndes & his Assigns during the life time of him and of Hugh Watson of the Middle Temple and the longest liver, who are both said to be dead; the value of Clerk of the Common Pleas cannot be certainly known as it depends entirely on the Fees of the Office which have amounted to between three and four hundred pounds yearly for some time past, out of which the Clerk has always paid an Assistant £100 ₩' An. The Salary of the Clerk of the Crown is £25 ₩' An. paid out of his Majesty's Quit Rents & the Fees may be about as much. Also the Appointment of David Græme Esq$^r$ to supply the Vacancy.

EXTRACTS FROM THE PARISH REGISTER OF ST. MARY'S,
CAYOU, ST. KITTS.

*Baptisms at Christ Church, Nichola Town, in the Island of St. Christopher.*
1740. June 1.   Mary, daugh$^r$ of Will$^m$ & Mary Lowndes.
1744. Aug$^t$ 1.   John Taylor, son of Will$^m$ & Mary Lowndes.

*Burials at Christ Church, Nichola Town.*
1763. July 26.   Ruth Lowndes, widow of Charles Lowndes.

*Marriages at Christ Church, Nichola Town.*
1739. Ap. 7.   Married Will$^m$ Lowndes & Mary d$^r$ of Nich$^s$ & Mary Taylor.

I hereby certify that the above statement of Baptisms, Burial & Marriage are correct Extracts from the Register Book of Baptisms, Burials and Marriages transcribed in 1787 by consent of the authorities in the Island, from the Original Registry, "which was in many places torn & defaced," & certified by the then Rector, Joseph Barnes, to be a "faithful copy." The Register Book does not date further back than April 8$^{th}$ 1730.

St. Mary's Rectory,                       EBENEZER ELLIOTT
  Cayou, St. Kitts                   Rector of Christ Church Nichola Town
    Jan$^y$ 15$^{th}$ 1870                & St. Mary, Cayou, St. Kitt's

www.ingramcontent.com/pod-product-compliance
Lightning Source LLC
Chambersburg PA
CBHW020325090426
42735CB00009B/1410